GitOps Cookbook
Kubernetes Automation in Practice

Natale Vinto and Alex Soto Bueno

Beijing · Boston · Farnham · Sebastopol · Tokyo

GitOps Cookbook

by Natale Vinto and Alex Soto Bueno

Published by O'Reilly Media, Inc., 1005 Gravenstein Highway North, Sebastopol, CA 95472.

O'Reilly books may be purchased for educational, business, or sales promotional use. Online editions are also available for most titles (*http://oreilly.com*). For more information, contact our corporate/institutional sales department: 800-998-9938 or *corporate@oreilly.com*.

Acquisitions Editor: John Devins
Development Editor: Shira Evans
Production Editor: Kate Galloway
Copyeditor: Kim Cofer
Proofreader: Liz Wheeler

Indexer: nSight, Inc.
Interior Designer: David Futato
Cover Designer: Karen Montgomery
Illustrator: Kate Dullea

January 2023:   First Edition

Revision History for the First Edition

2023-01-03:   First Release

See *http://oreilly.com/catalog/errata.csp?isbn=9781492097471* for release details.

978-1-492-09747-1

[LSI]

To Alessia and Sofia, the most beautiful chapters of my life.
—Natale

[Ada i Alexandra] Sabeu que sou flipants, encara que sortiu del fang.
—Alex

Table of Contents

Foreword

A few years ago, during a trip to Milan for a Red Hat event, I ran into a passionate colleague at the Red Hat office. We spoke at length about how customers in Italy adopt containers to speed up application development on OpenShift. While his name slipped my mind at the time, his enthusiasm about the subject didn't, especially since he was also hospitable enough to take me to an espresso bar near the office to show me what real coffee tastes like. A while later, I was introduced to a developer advocate in a meeting who would speak at a conference about CI/CD using products like OpenShift Pipelines and OpenShift GitOps that my teams delivered at the time. At that moment, I instantly recognized Natale. Many who attended that talk thought it was insightful, given his firsthand grasp of challenges that customers experience when delivering applications and his hands-on approach to technology.

Application delivery is a complex process involving many systems and teams with numerous handoffs between these parties, often synonymous with delays and back-and-forth talks at each point. Automation has long been a key enabler for improving this process and has become particularly popular within the DevOps movement. Continuous integration, infrastructure as code, and numerous other practices became common in many organizations as they navigated their journey toward adopting DevOps.

More recently, and coinciding with the increased adoption of Kubernetes, GitOps as a blueprint for implementing a subset of DevOps practices has become an area I frequently get asked about. While neither the term nor the practices GitOps advocates are new, it does combine. It presents the existing knowledge in a workflow that is simple, easy to understand, and can be implemented in a standard way across many teams.

Although the path to adopting the GitOps workflow is simple and concrete, many technical choices need to be made to fit within each organization's security, compliance, operational, and other requirements. Therefore, I am particularly thrilled about the existence of this book and the practical guides it provides to assist these teams in making choices that are right for their applications, teams, and organizations.

—Siamak Sadeghianfar
Product Management, Red Hat

Preface

We wrote this book for builders. Whether you are a developer, DevOps engineer, site reliability engineer (SRE), or platform engineer dealing with Kubernetes, you are building some good stuff. We would like to share our experience from what we have learned in the field and in the community about the latest Kubernetes automation insights for pipelines and CI/CD workloads. The book contains a comprehensive list of the most popular available software and tools in the Kubernetes and cloud native ecosystem for this purpose. We aim to provide a list of practical recipes that might help your daily job or are worth exploring further. We are not sticking to a particular technology or project for implementing Kubernetes automation. However, we are opinionated on some of our choices to deliver a concise GitOps pathway.

The book is organized in sequential chapters, from the basics to advanced topics in the Kubernetes ecosystem, following the GitOps principles. We hope you'll find these recipes valuable and inspiring for your projects!

- Chapter 1 is an introduction to GitOps principles and why they are continuously becoming more common and essential for any new IT project.

- Chapter 2 covers the installation requirements to run these recipes in a Kubernetes cluster. Concepts and tools like Git, Container Registry, Container Runtime, and Kubernetes are necessary for this journey.

- Chapter 3 walks you through a complete overview of containers and why they are essential for application development and deployment today. Kubernetes is a container-orchestration platform; however, it doesn't build containers out of the box. Therefore, we'll provide a list of practical recipes for making container apps with the most popular tools available in the cloud native community.

- Chapter 4 gives you an overview of Kustomize, a popular tool for managing Kubernetes resources. Kustomize is interoperable, and you find it often used within CI/CD pipelines.

- Chapter 5 explores Helm, a trendy tool to package applications in Kubernetes. Helm is also a templating system that you can use to deploy apps in CI/CD workloads.

- Chapter 6 walks you through cloud native CI/CD systems for Kubernetes. It gives a comprehensive list of recipes for the continuous integration part with Tekton, the Kubernetes-native CI/CD system. Additionally, it also covers other tools such as Drone and GitHub Actions.

- Chapter 7 kicks off the pure GitOps part of the book as it sticks to the Continuous Deployment phase with Argo CD, a popular GitOps tool for Kubernetes.

- Chapter 8 goes into the advanced topics for GitOps with Argo CD, such as secrets management, progressive application delivery, and multicluster deployments. This concludes the most common use cases and architectures you will likely work with today and tomorrow following the GitOps approach.

Conventions Used in This Book

The following typographical conventions are used in this book:

Italic
: Indicates new terms, URLs, email addresses, filenames, and file extensions.

`Constant width`
: Used for program listings, as well as within paragraphs to refer to program elements such as variable or function names, databases, data types, environment variables, statements, and keywords.

`Constant width bold`
: Shows commands or other text that should be typed literally by the user.

`Constant width italic`
: Shows text that should be replaced with user-supplied values or by values determined by context.

 This element signifies a tip or suggestion.

 This element signifies a general note.

This element indicates a warning or caution.

Using Code Examples

Supplemental material (code examples, exercises, etc.) is available for download at *https://github.com/gitops-cookbook*.

If you have a technical question or a problem using the code examples, please send email to *bookquestions@oreilly.com*.

This book is here to help you get your job done. In general, if example code is offered with this book, you may use it in your programs and documentation. You do not need to contact us for permission unless you're reproducing a significant portion of the code. For example, writing a program that uses several chunks of code from this book does not require permission. Selling or distributing examples from O'Reilly books does require permission. Answering a question by citing this book and quoting example code does not require permission. Incorporating a significant amount of example code from this book into your product's documentation does require permission.

We appreciate, but generally do not require, attribution. An attribution usually includes the title, author, publisher, and ISBN. For example: "*GitOps Cookbook* by Natale Vinto and Alex Soto Bueno (O'Reilly). Copyright 2023 Natale Vinto and Alex Soto Bueno, 978-1-492-09747-1."

If you feel your use of code examples falls outside fair use or the permission given above, feel free to contact us at *permissions@oreilly.com*.

O'Reilly Online Learning

O'REILLY® For more than 40 years, *O'Reilly Media* has provided technology and business training, knowledge, and insight to help companies succeed.

Our unique network of experts and innovators share their knowledge and expertise through books, articles, and our online learning platform. O'Reilly's online learning platform gives you on-demand access to live training courses, in-depth learning paths, interactive coding environments, and a vast collection of text and video from O'Reilly and 200+ other publishers. For more information, visit *http://oreilly.com*.

How to Contact Us

Please address comments and questions concerning this book to the publisher:

O'Reilly Media, Inc.
1005 Gravenstein Highway North
Sebastopol, CA 95472
800-998-9938 (in the United States or Canada)
707-829-0515 (international or local)
707-829-0104 (fax)

We have a web page for this book, where we list errata, examples, and any additional information. You can access this page at *https://oreil.ly/gitops-cookbook*.

Email *bookquestions@oreilly.com* to comment or ask technical questions about this book.

For news and information about our books and courses, visit *https://oreilly.com*.

Find us on LinkedIn: *https://linkedin.com/company/oreilly-media*.

Follow us on Twitter: *https://twitter.com/oreillymedia*.

Watch us on YouTube: *https://youtube.com/oreillymedia*.

Acknowledgments

We both want to thank our tech reviewers Peter Miron and Andy Block for their accurate review that helped us improve the reading experience with this book. Thanks also to the people at O'Reilly who helped us during the whole writing cycle. Many thanks to our colleagues Aubrey Muhlach and Colleen Lobner for the great support with publishing this book. Thanks to Kamesh Sampath and all the people who helped us during the early release phases with comments and suggestions that we added to the book—your input is much appreciated!

Alex Soto

During these challenging times, I'd like to acknowledge Santa (aquest any sí), Uri (don't stop the music), Guiri (un ciclista), Gavina, Gabi (thanks for the support), and Edgar and Ester (life is good especially on Friday); my friends Edson, Sebi (the best fellow traveler), Burr (I learned a lot from you), Kamesh, and all the Red Hat developers team, we are the best.

Jonathan Vila, Abel Salgado, and Jordi Sola for the fantastic conversations about Java and Kubernetes.

Last but certainly not least, I'd like to acknowledge Anna for being here; my parents Mili and Ramon for buying my first computer; my daughters Ada and Alexandra, "sou les ninetes dels meus ulls."

Natale Vinto

Special thanks to Alessia for the patience and motivation that helped me while writing this book. And to my parents for everything they made for me, grazie mamma e papà, you are the best!

## CHAPTER 1

Introduction

With the advent of practices such as infrastructure as code (IaC), software development has pushed the boundaries of platforms where you can run applications. This becomes more frequent with programmable, API-driven platforms such as public clouds and open source infrastructure solutions. While some years ago developers were only focusing on application source code, today they also have the opportunity to code the infrastructure where their application will run. This gives control and enables automation, which significantly reduces lead time.

A good example is with Kubernetes, a popular open source container workload orchestration platform and the de facto standard for running production applications, either on public or private clouds. The openness and extensibility of the platform enables automation, which reduces risks of delivery and increases service quality. Furthermore, this powerful paradigm is extended by another increasingly popular approach called GitOps.

1.1 What Is GitOps?

GitOps is a methodology and practice that uses Git repositories as a single source of truth to deliver infrastructure as code. It takes the pillars and approaches from DevOps culture and provides a framework to start realizing the results. The relationship between DevOps and GitOps is close, as GitOps has become the popular choice to implement and enhance DevOps, platform engineering, and SRE.

GitOps is an agnostic approach, and a GitOps framework can be built with tools such as Git, Kubernetes, and CI/CD solutions. The three main pillars of GitOps are:

- Git is the single source of truth
- Treat everything as code

- Operations are performed through Git workflows

There is an active community around GitOps, and the GitOps Working Group (*https://oreil.ly/FUbBy*) defines a set of GitOps Principles (currently in version 1.0.0) available at OpenGitOps (*https://opengitops.dev*):

Declarative
A system managed by GitOps must have its desired state expressed declaratively.

Versioned and immutable
The desired state is stored in a way that enforces immutability and versioning and retains a complete version history.

Pulled automatically
Software agents automatically pull the desired state declarations from the source.

Continuously reconciled
Software agents continuously observe the actual system state and attempt to apply the desired state.

1.2 Why GitOps?

Using the common Git-based workflows that developers are familiar with, GitOps expands upon existing processes from application development to deployment, app lifecycle management, and infrastructure configuration.

Every change throughout the application lifecycle is traced in the Git repository and is auditable. This approach is beneficial for both developers and operations teams as it enhances the ability to trace and reproduce issues quickly, improving overall security. One key point is to reduce the risk of unwanted changes (drift) and correct them before they go into production.

Here is a summary of the benefits of the GitOps adoption in four key aspects:

Standard workflow
Use familiar tools and Git workflows from application development teams

Enhanced security
Review changes beforehand, detect configuration drifts, and take action

Visibility and audit
Capture and trace any change to clusters through Git history

Multicluster consistency
Reliably and consistently configure multiple environments and multiple Kubernetes clusters and deployment

1.3 Kubernetes CI/CD

Continuous integration (CI) and continuous delivery (CD) are methods used to frequently deliver apps by introducing automation into the stages of app development. CI/CD pipelines are one of the most common use cases for GitOps.

In a typical CI/CD pipeline, submitted code checks the CI process while the CD process checks and applies requirements for things like security, infrastructure as code, or any other boundaries set for the application framework. All code changes are tracked, making updates easy while also providing version control should a rollback be needed. CD is the GitOps domain and it works together with the CI part to deploy apps in multiple environments, as you can see in Figure 1-1.

Build	Test	Security Checks	Release	Deploy Stage	Deploy Prod

Continuous Integration

Continuous Delivery

Figure 1-1. Continuous integration and continuous delivery

With Kubernetes, it's easy to implement an in-cluster CI/CD pipeline. You can have CI software create the container image representing your application and store it in a container image registry. Afterward, a Git workflow such as a pull request can change the Kubernetes manifests illustrating the deployment of your apps and start a CD sync loop, as shown in Figure 1-2.

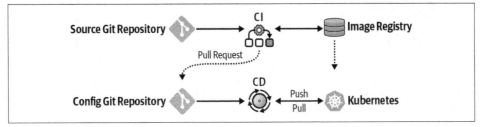

Figure 1-2. Application deployment model

This cookbook will show practical recipes for implementing this model on Kubernetes acting as a CI/CD and GitOps platform.

1.4 App Deployment with GitOps on Kubernetes

As GitOps is an agnostic, platform-independent approach, the application deployment model on Kubernetes can be either in-cluster or multicluster. An external GitOps tool can use Kubernetes just as a target platform for deploying apps. At the same time, in-cluster approaches run a GitOps engine inside Kubernetes to deploy apps and sync manifests in one or more Kubernetes clusters.

The GitOps engine takes care of the CD part of the CI/CD pipeline and accomplishes a GitOps loop, which is composed of four main actions as shown in Figure 1-3:

Deploy
> Deploy the manifests from Git.

Monitor
> Monitor either the Git repo or the cluster state.

Detect drift
> Detect any change from what is described in Git and what is present in the cluster.

Take action
> Perform an action that reflects what is on Git (rollback or three-way diff). Git is the source of truth, and any change is performed via a Git workflow.

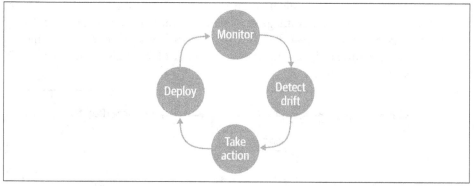

Figure 1-3. GitOps loop

In Kubernetes, application deployment using the GitOps approach makes use of at least two Git repositories: one for the app source code, and one for the Kubernetes manifests describing the app's deployment (Deployment, Service, etc.).

Figure 1-4 illustrates the structure of a GitOps project on Kubernetes.

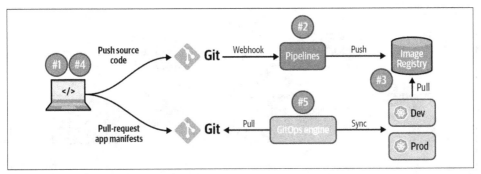

Figure 1-4. Kubernetes GitOps loop

The following list outlines the items in the workflow:

1. App source code repository
2. CI pipeline creating a container image
3. Container image registry
4. Kubernetes manifests repository
5. GitOps engine syncing manifests to one or more clusters and detecting drifts

1.5 DevOps and Agility

GitOps is a developer-centric approach to continuous delivery and infrastructure operations, and a developer workflow through Git for automating processes. As DevOps is complementary to Agile software development, GitOps is complementary to DevOps for infrastructure automation and application lifecycle management. As you can see in Figure 1-5, it's a developer workflow for automating operations.

One of the most critical aspects of the Agile methodology is to reduce the lead time (*https://oreil.ly/r52pg*), which is described more abstractly as the time elapsed between identifying a requirement and its fulfillment.

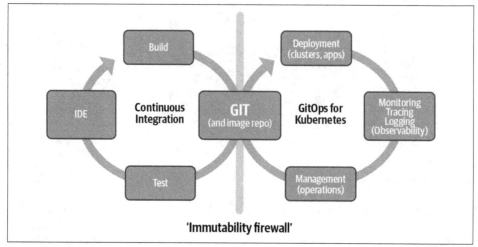

Figure 1-5. GitOps development cycle

Reducing this time is fundamental and requires a cultural change in IT organizations. Seeing applications live provides developers with a feedback loop to redesign and improve their code and make their projects thrive. Similarly to DevOps, GitOps also requires a cultural adoption in business processes. Every operation, such as application deployment or infrastructure change, is only possible through Git workflows. And sometimes, this means a cultural shift.

The "Teaching Elephants to Dance (and Fly!)" (*https://oreil.ly/gPja9*) speech from Burr Sutter gives a clear idea of the context. The elephant is where your organization is today. There are phases of change between traditional and modern environments powered by GitOps tools. Some organizations have the luxury of starting from scratch, but for many businesses, the challenge is teaching their lumbering elephant to dance like a graceful ballerina.

## CHAPTER 2

Requirements

This book is about GitOps and Kubernetes, and as such, you'll need a container registry to publish the containers built throughout the book (see Recipe 2.1).

Also, a Git service is required to implement GitOps methodologies; you'll learn how to register to public Git services like GitHub or GitLab (see Recipe 2.2).

Finally, it would be best to have a Kubernetes cluster to run the book examples. Although we'll show you how to install Minikube as a Kubernetes cluster (see Recipe 2.3), and the book is tested with Minikube, any Kubernetes installation should work as well.

Let's prepare your laptop to execute the recipes provided in this book.

2.1 Registering for a Container Registry

Problem

You want to create an account for a container registry service so you can store generated containers.

Solution

You may need to publish some containers into a public container registry as you work through this book. Use Docker Hub (`docker.io`) to publish containers.

If you already have an account with `docker.io`, you can skip the following steps. Otherwise, keep reading to learn how to sign up for an account.

Discussion

Visit DockerHub (*https://hub.docker.com*) to sign up for an account. The page should be similar to Figure 2-1.

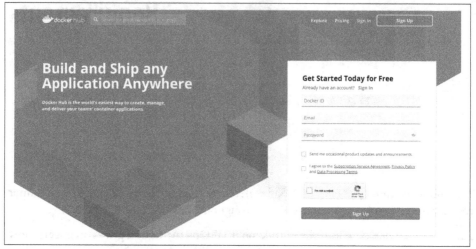

Figure 2-1. DockerHub registration page

When the page is loaded, fill in the form by setting a Docker ID, Email, and Password, and click the Sign Up button.

When you are registered and your account confirmed, you'll be ready to publish containers under the previous step's Docker ID.

See Also

Another popular container registry service is quay.io. It can be used on the cloud (like docker.io) or installed on-premises.

Visit the website (*https://quay.io*) to get more information about Quay. The page should be similar to Figure 2-2.

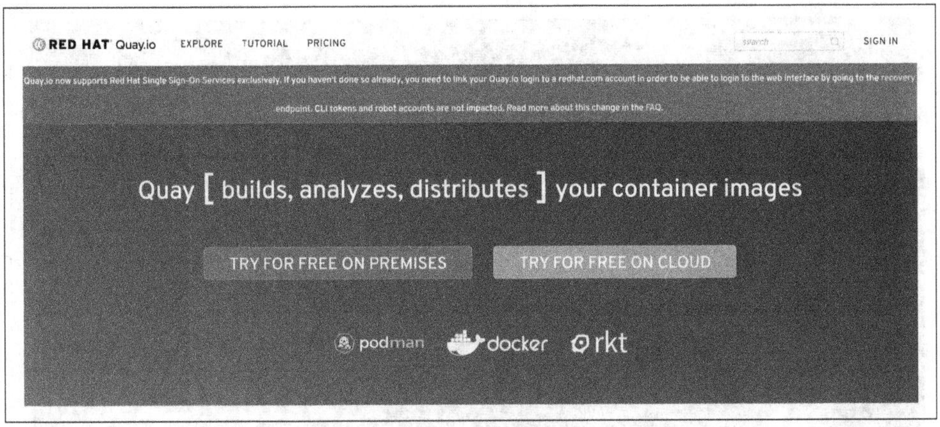

Figure 2-2. Quay registration page

2.2 Registering for a Git Repository

Problem

You want to create an account for a Git service so you can store source code in a repository.

Solution

You may need to publish some source code into a public Git service in this book. Use GitHub as a Git service to create and fork Git repositories.

If you already have an account with GitHub, you can skip the following steps, otherwise keep reading to learn how to sign up for an account.

Discussion

Visit the GitHub web page (*https://github.com*) to sign up for an account. The page should be similar to Figure 2-3.

Figure 2-3. GitHub welcome page to register

When the page is loaded, click the Sign up for GitHub button (see Figure 2-3) and follow the instructions. The Sign in page should be similar to Figure 2-4.

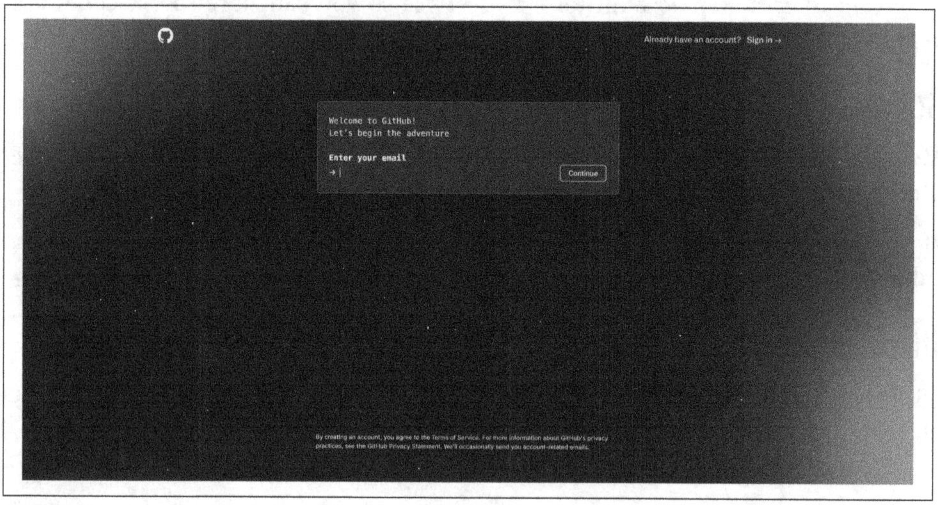

Figure 2-4. Sign In GitHub page

When you are registered and your account confirmed, you'll be ready to start creating or forking Git repositories into your GitHub account.

Also, you'll need to fork the book source code repository (*https://oreil.ly/uqjTA*) into your account. Click the Fork button shown in Figure 2-5.

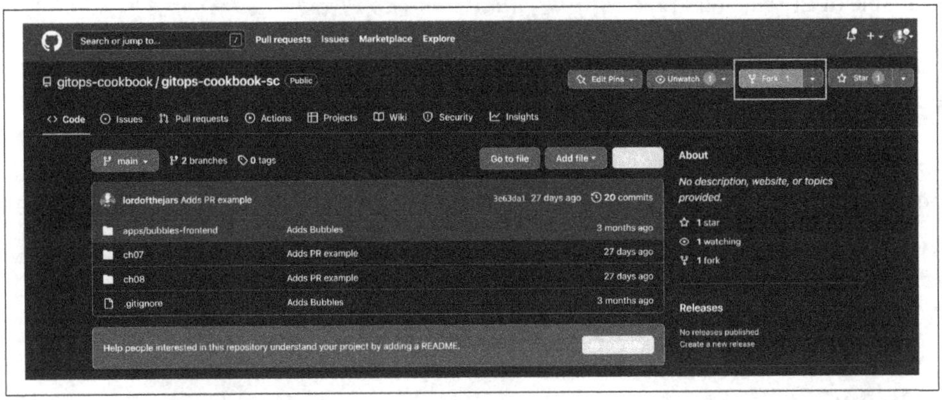

Figure 2-5. Fork button

Then select your account in the Owner section, if not selected yet, and click the button "Create fork" button as shown in Figure 2-6.

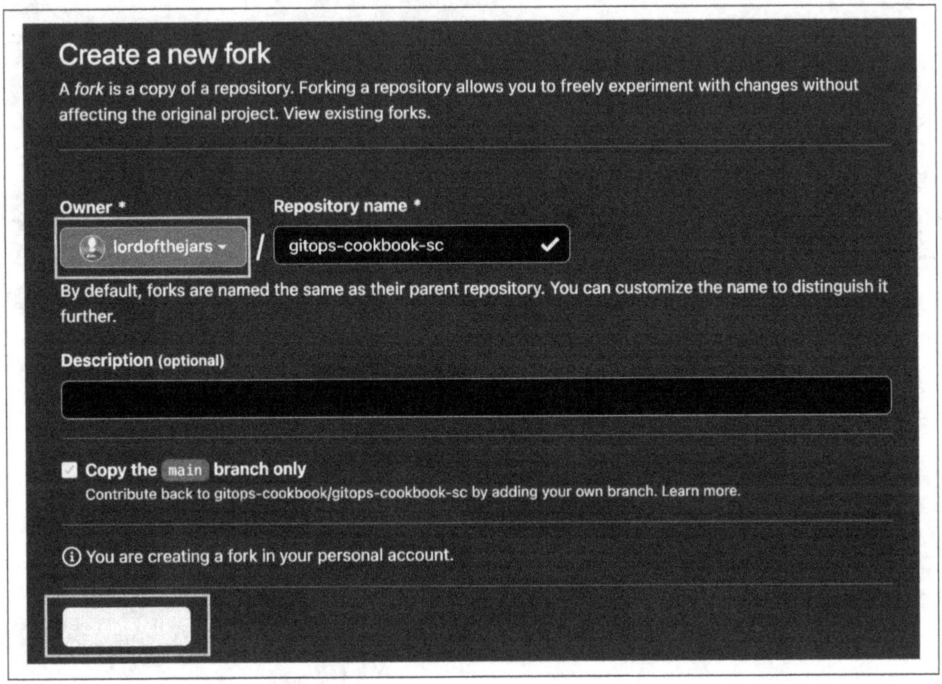

Figure 2-6. Create fork button

To follow along with the example in the following chapters, you can clone this book's repositories locally. When not mentioned explicitly, we will refer to the examples available in the chapters repo (*https://github.com/gitops-cookbook/chapters*):

```
git clone https://github.com/gitops-cookbook/chapters
```

See Also

Another popular Git service is GitLab. It can be used on the cloud or installed on-premises.

Visit GitLab (*https://about.gitlab.com*) for more information.

2.3 Creating a Local Kubernetes Cluster

Problem

You want to spin up a Kubernetes cluster locally.

Solution

In this book, you may need a Kubernetes cluster to run most recipes. Use Minikube to spin up a Kubernetes cluster in your local machine.

Discussion

Minikube uses container/virtualization technology like Docker, Podman, Hyperkit, Hyper-V, KVM, or VirtualBox to boot up a Linux machine with a Kubernetes cluster installed inside.

For simplicity and to use an installation that will work in most of the platforms, we are going to use VirtualBox as a virtualization system.

To install VirtualBox (if you haven't done it yet), visit the home page (*https://oreil.ly/ T93oU*) and click the Download link as shown in Figure 2-7.

 For those using macOS, the following instructions have been tested on a Mac AMD64 with macOS Monterey and VirtualBox 6.1. At the time of writing this book, there were some incompatibilities when using the ARM version or macOS Ventura.

Figure 2-7. VirtualBox home page

Select the package based on the operating system, download it, and install it on your computer. After installing VirtualBox (we used the 6.1.x version), the next step is to download and spin up a cluster using Minikube.

Visit the GitHub repo (*https://oreil.ly/mmwVP*), unfold the Assets section, and download the Minikube file that matches your platform specification. For example, in the case of an AMD Mac, you should select *minikube-darwin-amd64* as shown in Figure 2-8.

Uncompress the file (if necessary) and copy it with the name *minikube* in a directory accessible by the `PATH` environment variable such as (`/usr/local/bin`) in Linux or macOS.

With VirtualBox and Minikube installed, we can spin up a Kubernetes cluster in the local machine. Let's install Kubernetes version 1.23.0 as it was the latest version at the time of writing (although any other previous versions can be used as well).

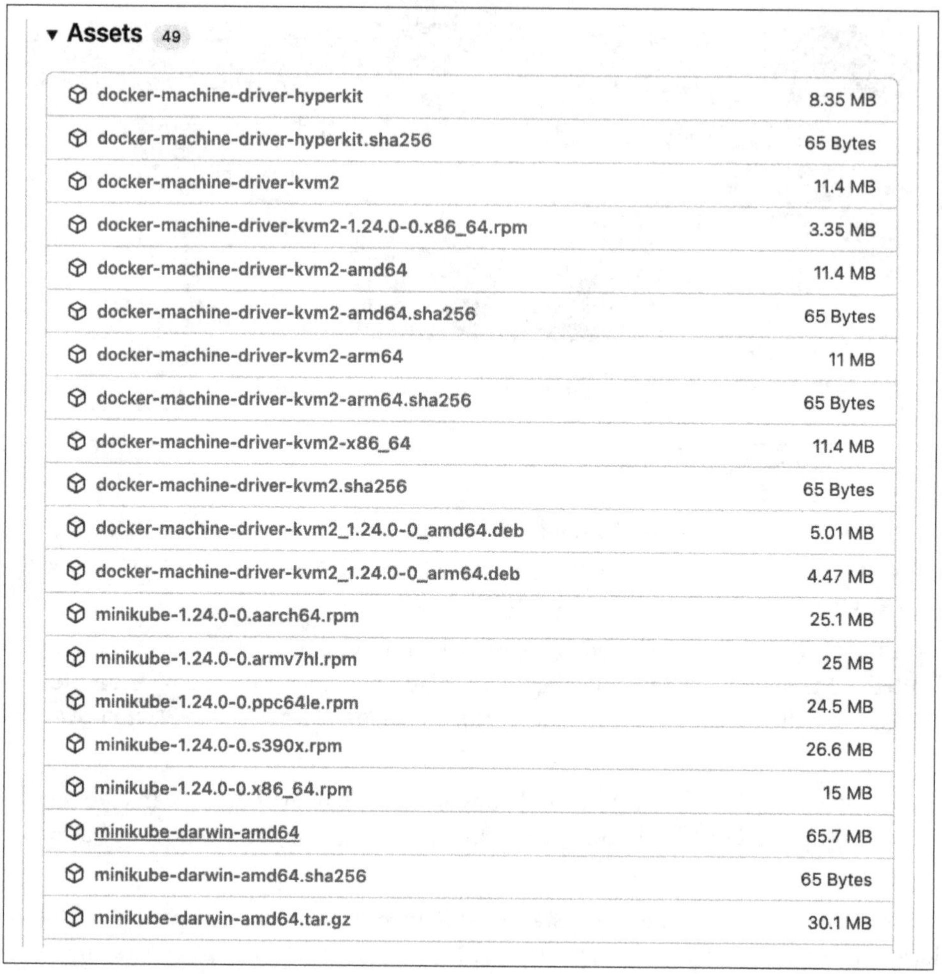

⬡ docker-machine-driver-hyperkit	8.35 MB
⬡ docker-machine-driver-hyperkit.sha256	65 Bytes
⬡ docker-machine-driver-kvm2	11.4 MB
⬡ docker-machine-driver-kvm2-1.24.0-0.x86_64.rpm	3.35 MB
⬡ docker-machine-driver-kvm2-amd64	11.4 MB
⬡ docker-machine-driver-kvm2-amd64.sha256	65 Bytes
⬡ docker-machine-driver-kvm2-arm64	11 MB
⬡ docker-machine-driver-kvm2-arm64.sha256	65 Bytes
⬡ docker-machine-driver-kvm2-x86_64	11.4 MB
⬡ docker-machine-driver-kvm2.sha256	65 Bytes
⬡ docker-machine-driver-kvm2_1.24.0-0_amd64.deb	5.01 MB
⬡ docker-machine-driver-kvm2_1.24.0-0_arm64.deb	4.47 MB
⬡ minikube-1.24.0-0.aarch64.rpm	25.1 MB
⬡ minikube-1.24.0-0.armv7hl.rpm	25 MB
⬡ minikube-1.24.0-0.ppc64le.rpm	24.5 MB
⬡ minikube-1.24.0-0.s390x.rpm	26.6 MB
⬡ minikube-1.24.0-0.x86_64.rpm	15 MB
⬡ minikube-darwin-amd64	65.7 MB
⬡ minikube-darwin-amd64.sha256	65 Bytes
⬡ minikube-darwin-amd64.tar.gz	30.1 MB

Figure 2-8. Minikube release page

Run the following command in a terminal window to spin up the Kubernetes cluster with 8 GB of memory assigned:

```
minikube start --kubernetes-version='v1.23.0' /
--driver='virtualbox' --memory=8196 -p gitops ❶ ❷ ❸
```

❶ Creates a Kubernetes cluster with version 1.23.0

❷ Uses VirtualBox as virtualization tool

❸ Creates a profile name (`gitops`) to the cluster to refer to it later

The output lines should be similar to:

```
[gitops] Minikube v1.24.0 on Darwin 12.0.1
 Using the virtualbox driver based on user configuration
Starting control plane node gitops in cluster gitops ❶
Creating virtualbox VM (CPUs=2, Memory=8196MB, Disk=20000MB) ...
    > kubeadm.sha256: 64 B / 64 B [-------------------------] 100.00% ? p/s 0s
    > kubelet.sha256: 64 B / 64 B [-------------------------] 100.00% ? p/s 0s
    > kubectl.sha256: 64 B / 64 B [-------------------------] 100.00% ? p/s 0s
    > kubeadm: 43.11 MiB / 43.11 MiB [---------------] 100.00% 3.46 MiB p/s 13s
    > kubectl: 44.42 MiB / 44.42 MiB [---------------] 100.00% 3.60 MiB p/s 13s
    > kubelet: 118.73 MiB / 118.73 MiB [-------------] 100.00% 6.32 MiB p/s 19s

    • Generating certificates and keys ...
    • Booting up control plane ... ❷
    • Configuring RBAC rules ...
    • Using image gcr.io/k8s-minikube/storage-provisioner:v5
...

    Verifying Kubernetes components...
Enabled addons: storage-provisioner, default-storageclass

 /usr/local/bin/kubectl is version 1.21.0, which
may have incompatibilites with Kubernetes 1.23.0. ❸
    • Want kubectl v1.23.0? Try 'minikube kubectl -- get pods -A'
Done! kubectl is now configured to use "gitops" cluster and
 "default" namespace by default ❹
```

❶ Starts the gitops cluster

❷ Boots up the Kubernetes cluster control plane

❸ Detects that we have an old kubectl tool

❹ Cluster is up and running

To align the Kubernetes cluster and Kubernetes CLI tool version, you can download the kubectl 1.23.0 version running from *https://dl.k8s.io/release/v1.23.0/bin/darwin/amd64/kubectl*.

 You need to change darwin/amd64 to your specific architecture. For example, in Windows it might be windows/amd64/kubectl.exe.

Copy the kubectl CLI tool in a directory accessible by the PATH environment variable such as (/usr/local/bin) in Linux or macOS.

See Also

There are other ways to run Kubernetes in a local machine.

One that is very popular is kind (*https://oreil.ly/8B2bH*).

Although the examples in this book should work in any Kubernetes implementation as only standard resources are used, we've only tested with Minikube.

## CHAPTER 3

Containers

Containers are a popular and standard format for packaging applications. The format is an open standard promoted by the Open Container Initiative (OCI) (*https://open containers.org*), an open governance structure for the express purpose of creating open industry standards around container formats and runtimes. The openness of this format ensures portability and interoperability across different operating systems, vendors, platforms, or clouds. Kubernetes runs containerized apps, so before going into the GitOps approach to managing apps on Kubernetes, we provide a list of recipes useful for understanding how to package your application as a container image.

The first step for creating images is to use a container engine for packaging your application by building a layered structure containing a base OS and additional layers on top such as runtimes, libraries, and applications. Docker is a widespread open source implementation of a container engine and runtime, and it can generate a container image by specifying a manifest called a Dockerfile (see Recipe 3.1).

Since the format is open, it's possible to create container images with other tools. Docker (*https://www.docker.com*), a popular container engine, requires the installation and the execution of a *daemon* that can handle all the operations with the container engine. Developers can use a software development kit (SDK) to interact with the Docker daemon or use *dockerless* solutions such as JiB to create container images (see Recipe 3.2).

If you don't want to rely on a specific programming language or SDK to build container images, you can use another *daemonless* solution like Buildah (see Recipe 3.3) or Buildpacks (see Recipe 3.4). Those are other popular open source tools for building OCI container images. By avoiding dependencies from the OS, such tools make automation more manageable and portable (see Chapter 6).

Kubernetes doesn't provide a native mechanism for building container images. However, its highly extensible architecture allows interoperability with external tools and the platform's extensibility to create container images. Shipwright is an open source framework for building container images on Kubernetes, providing an abstraction that can use tools such as kaniko, Buildpacks, or Buildah (see Recipe 3.5) to create container images.

At the end of this chapter, you'll learn how to create OCI-compliant container images from a Dockerfile, either from a host with Docker installed, or using tools such as Buildah and Buildpacks.

3.1 Building a Container Using Docker

Problem

You want to create a container image for your application with Docker.

Solution

The first thing you need to do is install Docker (*https://oreil.ly/jd0kH*).

 Docker is available for Mac, Windows, and Linux. Download the installer for your operating system and refer to the documentation (*https://oreil.ly/7vGmZ*) to start the Docker service.

Developers can create a container image by defining a *Dockerfile*. The best definition for a Dockerfile comes from the Docker documentation (*https://oreil.ly/RMm2y*) itself: "A Dockerfile is a text document that contains all the commands a user could call on the command line to assemble an image."

Container images present a layered structure, as you can see in Figure 3-1. Each container image provides the foundation layer for a container, and any update is just an additional layer that can be committed on the foundation.

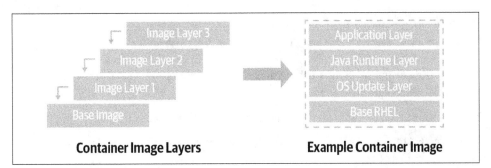

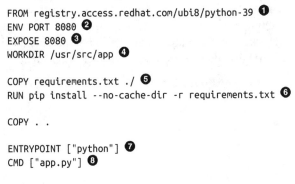

Container Image Layers   **Example Container Image**

Figure 3-1. Container image layers

You can create a Dockerfile like the one shown here, which will generate a container image for Python apps. You can also find this example in this book's repository (*https://oreil.ly/J7cXP*).

```
FROM registry.access.redhat.com/ubi8/python-39 ❶
ENV PORT 8080 ❷
EXPOSE 8080 ❸
WORKDIR /usr/src/app ❹

COPY requirements.txt ./ ❺
RUN pip install --no-cache-dir -r requirements.txt ❻

COPY . .

ENTRYPOINT ["python"] ❼
CMD ["app.py"] ❽
```

❶ FROM: always start from a base image as a foundational layer. In this case we start from a Universal Base Image (UBI), publicly available based on RHEL 8 with Python 3.9 runtime.

❷ ENV: set an environment variable for the app.

❸ EXPOSE: expose a port to the container network, in this case port TCP 8080.

❹ WORKDIR: set a directory inside the container to work with.

❺ COPY: copy the assets from the source code files on your workstation to the container image layer, in this case, to the WORKDIR.

❻ RUN: run a command inside the container, using the tools already available within the base image. In this case, it runs the pip tool to install dependencies.

❼ ENTRYPOINT: define the entry point for your app inside the container. It can be a binary or a script. In this case, it runs the Python interpreter.

❽ CMD: the command that is used when starting a container. In this case it uses the name of the Python app app.py.

You can now create your container image with the following command:

```
docker build -f Dockerfile -t quay.io/gitops-cookbook/pythonapp:latest
```

 Change the container image name with the your registry, user, and repo. Example: quay.io/youruser/yourrepo:latest. See Chapter 2 for how to create a new account on registries such as Quay.io.

Your container image is building now. Docker will fetch existing layers from a public container registry (DockerHub, Quay, Red Hat Registry, etc.) and add a new layer with the content specified in the Dockerfile. Such layers could also be available locally, if already downloaded, in special storage called a *container cache* or *Docker cache*.

```
STEP 1: FROM registry.access.redhat.com/ubi8/python-39
Getting image source signatures
Copying blob adffa6963146 done
Copying blob 4125bdfaec5e done
Copying blob 362566a15abb done
Copying blob 0661f10c38cc done
Copying blob 26f1167feaf7 done
Copying config a531ae7675 done
Writing manifest to image destination
Storing signatures
STEP 2: ENV PORT 8080
--> 6dbf4ac027e
STEP 3: EXPOSE 8080
--> f78357fe402
STEP 4: WORKDIR /usr/src/app
--> 547bf8ca5c5
STEP 5: COPY requirements.txt ./
--> 456cab38c97
STEP 6: RUN pip install --no-cache-dir -r requirements.txt
Collecting Flask
  Downloading Flask-2.0.2-py3-none-any.whl (95 kB)
     |████████████████████████████████| 95 kB 10.6 MB/s
Collecting itsdangerous>=2.0
  Downloading itsdangerous-2.0.1-py3-none-any.whl (18 kB)
Collecting Werkzeug>=2.0
  Downloading Werkzeug-2.0.2-py3-none-any.whl (288 kB)
     |████████████████████████████████| 288 kB 1.7 MB/s
Collecting click>=7.1.2
  Downloading click-8.0.3-py3-none-any.whl (97 kB)
     |████████████████████████████████| 97 kB 31.9 MB/s
```

```
Collecting Jinja2>=3.0
  Downloading Jinja2-3.0.3-py3-none-any.whl (133 kB)
     |████████████████████████████| 133 kB 38.8 MB/s
STEP 7: COPY . .
--> 3e6b73464eb
STEP 8: ENTRYPOINT ["python"]
--> acabca89260
STEP 9: CMD ["app.py"]
STEP 10: COMMIT quay.io/gitops-cookbook/pythonapp:latest
--> 52e134d39af
52e134d39af013a25f3e44d25133478dc20b46626782762f4e46b1ff6f0243bb
```

Your container image is now available in your Docker cache and ready to be used. You can verify its presence with this command:

```
docker images
```

You should get the list of available container images from the cache in output. Those could be images you have built or downloaded with the docker pull command:

```
REPOSITORY                          TAG      IMAGE ID      CREATED↳
    SIZE
quay.io/gitops-cookbook/pythonapp   latest   52e134d39af0  6 minutes ago↳
    907 MB
```

Once your image is created, you can consume it locally or push it to a public container registry to be consumed elsewhere, like from a CI/CD pipeline.

You need to first log in to your public registry. In this example, we are using Quay:

```
docker login quay.io
```

You should get output similar to this:

```
Login Succeeded!
```

Then you can push your container image to the registry:

```
docker push quay.io/gitops-cookbook/pythonapp:latest
```

As confirmed, you should get output similar to this:

```
Getting image source signatures
Copying blob e6e8a2c58ac5 done
Copying blob 3ba8c926eef9 done
Copying blob 558b534f4e1b done
Copying blob 25f82e0f4ef5 done
Copying blob 7b17276847a2 done
Copying blob 352ba846236b done
Copying blob 2de82c390049 done
Copying blob 26525e00a8d8 done
Copying config 52e134d39a done
Writing manifest to image destination
Copying config 52e134d39a [--------------------------------------] 0.0b / 5.4KiB
Writing manifest to image destination
Storing signatures
```

Discussion

You can create container images in this way with Docker from your workstation or any host where the Docker service/daemon is running.

Additionally, you can use functionalities offered by a public registry such as Quay.io that can directly create the container image from a Dockerfile and store it to the registry.

The build requires access to all layers, thus an internet connection to the registries storing base layers is needed, or at least having them in the container cache. Docker has a layered structure where any change to your app is committed on top of the existing layers, so there's no need to download all the layers each time since it will add only deltas for each new change.

Container images typically start from a base OS layer such as Fedora, CentOS, Ubuntu, Alpine, etc. However, they can also start from scratch, an empty layer for super-minimal images containing only the app's binary. See the scratch documentation (*https://oreil.ly/vj0gs*) for more info.

If you want to run your previously created container image, you can do so with this command:

```
docker run -p 8080:8080 -ti quay.io/gitops-cookbook/pythonapp:latest
```

docker run has many options to start your container. The most common are:

-p

Binds the port of the container with the port of the host running such container.

-t

Attaches a TTY to the container.

-i

Goes into an interactive mode.

-d

Goes in the background, printing a hash that you can use to interact asynchronously with the running container.

The preceding command will start your app in the Docker network and bind it to port 8080 of your workstation:

```
* Serving Flask app 'app' (lazy loading)
* Environment: production
  WARNING: This is a development server. Do not use it in a production deployment.
  Use a production WSGI server instead.
* Debug mode: on
* Running on all addresses.
  WARNING: This is a development server. Do not use it in a production deployment.
* Running on http://10.0.2.100:8080/ (Press CTRL+C to quit)
* Restarting with stat
* Debugger is active!
* Debugger PIN: 103-809-567
```

From a new terminal, try accessing your running container:

```
curl http://localhost:8080
```

You should get output like this:

```
Hello, World!
```

See Also

- Best practices for writing Dockerfiles (*https://oreil.ly/2hMQD*)
- Manage Docker images (*https://oreil.ly/hUByf*)

3.2 Building a Container Using Dockerless Jib

Problem

You are a software developer, and you want to create a container image without installing Docker or any additional software on your workstation.

Solution

As discussed in Recipe 3.1, you need to install the Docker engine to create container images. Docker requires permissions to install a service running as a daemon, thus a privileged process in your operating system. Today, *dockerless* solutions are also available for developers; a popular one is Jib.

Jib (*https://oreil.ly/NYCtv*) is an open source framework for Java made by Google to build OCI-compliant container images, without the need for Docker or any container runtime. Jib comes as a library that Java developers can import in their Maven or Gradle projects. This means you can create a container image for your app without writing or maintaining any Dockerfiles, delegating this complexity to Jib.

We see the benefits from this approach as the following:[1]

Pure Java
> No Docker or Dockerfile knowledge is required. Simply add Jib as a plug-in, and it will generate the container image for you.

Speed
> The application is divided into multiple layers, splitting dependencies from classes. There's no need to rebuild the container image like for Dockerfiles; Jib takes care of modifying the layers that changed.

Reproducibility
> Unnecessary updates are not triggered because the same contents generate the same image.

The easiest way to kickstart a container image build with Jib on existing Maven is by adding the plug-in via the command line:

```
mvn compile com.google.cloud.tools:jib-maven-plugin:3.2.0:build -Dimage=<MY IMAGE>
```

Alternatively, you can do so by adding Jib as a plug-in into your *pom.xml*:

```
<project>
  ...
  <build>
    <plugins>
      ...
      <plugin>
        <groupId>com.google.cloud.tools</groupId>
        <artifactId>jib-maven-plugin</artifactId>
        <version>3.2.0</version>
        <configuration>
          <to>
            <image>myimage</image>
          </to>
        </configuration>
      </plugin>
      ...
    </plugins>
  </build>
  ...
</project>
```

In this way, you can also manage other settings such as authentication or parameters for the build.

Let's now add Jib to an existing Java application, a Hello World application in Spring Boot that you can find in the book's repository (*https://oreil.ly/dn1LF*).

---

1 For a presentation about Jib, see Appu Goundan and Qingyang Chen's presentation from Velocity San Jose 2018 (*https://oreil.ly/W4j49*).

Run the following command to create a container image without using Docker, and push it directly to a container registry. In this example, we use Quay.io, and we will store the container image at *quay.io/gitops-cookbook/jib-example:latest*, so you will need to provide your credentials for the registry:

```
mvn compile com.google.cloud.tools:jib-maven-plugin:3.2.0:build \
-Dimage=quay.io/gitops-cookbook/jib-example:latest \
-Djib.to.auth.username=<USERNAME> \
-Djib.to.auth.password=<PASSWORD>
```

The authentication here is handled with command-line options, but Jib can manage existing authentication with Docker CLI or read credentials from your *settings.xml* file.

The build takes a few moments, and the result is a Java-specific container image, based on the *adoptOpenJDK* base image, built locally and pushed directly to a registry. In this case, to Quay.io:

```
[INFO] Scanning for projects...
[INFO]
[INFO] ----------------------< com.redhat:hello >----------------------
[INFO] Building hello 0.0.1-SNAPSHOT
[INFO] --------------------------------[ jar ]--------------------------------
...
[INFO] Containerizing application to quay.io/gitops-cookbook/jib-example...
[INFO] Using credentials from <to><auth> for quay.io/gitops-cookbook/jib-example
[INFO] The base image requires auth. Trying again for eclipse-temurin:11-jre...
[INFO] Using base image with digest:↳
  sha256:83d92ee225e443580cc3685ef9574582761cf975abc53850c2bc44ec47d7d9430]
[INFO]
[INFO] Container entrypoint set to [java, -cp, @/app/jib-classpath-file,↳
  com.redhat.hello.HelloApplication]FO]
[INFO]
[INFO] Built and pushed image as quay.io/gitops-cookbook/jib-example
[INFO] Executing tasks:
[INFO] [============================] 100,0% complete
[INFO]
[INFO] --------------------------------------------------------------------
[INFO] BUILD SUCCESS
[INFO] --------------------------------------------------------------------
[INFO] Total time:  41.366 s
[INFO] Finished at: 2022-01-25T19:04:09+01:00
[INFO] --------------------------------------------------------------------
```

 If you have Docker and run the command docker images, you won't see this image in your local cache!

Discussion

Your container image is not present in your local cache, as you don't need any container runtime to build images with Jib. You won't see it with the docker images command, but you can pull it from the public container registry afterward, and it will store it in your cache.

This approach is suitable for development velocity and automation, where the CI system doesn't need to have Docker installed on the nodes where it runs. Jib can create the container image without any Dockerfiles. Additionally, it can push the image to a container registry.

If you also want to store it locally from the beginning, Jib can connect to Docker hosts and do it for you.

You can pull your container image from the registry to try it:

```
docker run -p 8080:8080 -ti quay.io/gitops-cookbook/jib-example

Trying to pull quay.io/gitops-cookbook/jib-example:latest...
Getting image source signatures
Copying blob ea362f368469 done
Copying blob d5cc550bb6a0 done
Copying blob bcc17963ea24 done
Copying blob 9b46d5d971fa done
Copying blob 51f4f7c353f0 done
Copying blob 43b2cdfa19bb done
Copying blob fd142634d578 done
Copying blob 78c393914c97 done
Copying config 346462b8d3 done
Writing manifest to image destination
Storing signatures


  .   ____          _            __ _ _
 /\\ / ___'_ __ _ _(_)_ __  __ _ \ \ \ \
( ( )\___ | '_ | '_| | '_ \/ _` | \ \ \ \
 \\/  ___)| |_)| | | | | || (_| |  ) ) ) )
  '  |____| .__|_| |_|_| |_\__, | / / / /
 =========|_|==============|___/=/_/_/_/
 :: Spring Boot ::                (v2.6.3)

2022-01-25 18:36:24.762  INFO 1 --- [ main] com.redhat.hello.HelloApplication↳
        : Starting HelloApplication using Java 11.0.13 on a719cf76f440 with PID 1↳
        (/app/classes started by root in /)
2022-01-25 18:36:24.765  INFO 1 --- [ main] com.redhat.hello.HelloApplication↳
        : No active profile set, falling back to default profiles: default
2022-01-25 18:36:25.700  INFO 1 --- [ main] o.s.b.w.embedded.tomcat.TomcatWeb-
Server↳
    : Tomcat initialized with port(s): 8080 (http)
2022-01-25 18:36:25.713  INFO 1 --- [ main] o.apache.catalina.core.StandardSer-
vice↳
    : Starting service [Tomcat]
2022-01-25 18:36:25.713  INFO 1 --- [ main] org.apache.catalina.core.StandardEn-
```

```
gine↳
    : Starting Servlet engine: [Apache Tomcat/9.0.56]
2022-01-25 18:36:25.781  INFO 1 --- [ main] o.a.c.c.C.[Tomcat].[localhost].[/]↳
        : Initializing Spring embedded WebApplicationContext
2022-01-25 18:36:25.781  INFO 1 --- [ main] w.s.c.ServletWebServerApplicationCon-
text↳
    : Root WebApplicationContext: initialization completed in 947 ms
2022-01-25 18:36:26.087  INFO 1 --- [ main] o.s.b.w.embedded.tomcat.TomcatWeb-
Server↳
    : Tomcat started on port(s): 8080 (http) with context path ''
2022-01-25 18:36:26.096  INFO 1 --- [ main] com.redhat.hello.HelloApplication↳
        : Started HelloApplication in 1.778 seconds (JVM running for 2.177)
```

Get the `hello` endpoint:

```
curl localhost:8080/hello
```

```
{"id":1,"content":"Hello, World!"}
```

See Also

- Using Jib with Quarkus projects (*https://oreil.ly/sTcpJ*)

3.3 Building a Container Using Buildah

Problem

Sometimes installing or managing Docker is not possible. Dockerless solutions for creating container images are useful in use cases such as local development or CI/CD systems.

Solution

The OCI specification is an open standard, and this favors multiple open source implementations for the container engine and the container image building mechanism. Two growing popular examples today are Podman (*https://podman.io*) and Buildah (*https://buildah.io*).

 While Docker uses a single monolithic application for creating, running, and shipping container images, the codebase for container management functionalities here has been split between different projects like Podman, Buildah, and Skopeo. Podman support is already available on Mac and Windows, however Buildah is currently only available on Linux or Linux subsystems such as WSL2 for Windows. See the documentation (*https://oreil.ly/W9l1a*) to install it on your workstation.

Those are two complementary open source projects and command-line tools that work on OCI containers and images; however, they differ in their specialization. While Podman specializes in commands and functions that help you to maintain and modify container images, such as pulling, tagging, and pushing, Buildah specializes in building container images. Decoupling functions in different processes is done by design, as the authors wanted to move from the single privileged process Docker model to a lightweight, rootless, daemonless, and decoupled set of tools to improve agility and security.

> Following the same approach, you find Skopeo (*https://oreil.ly/ oJnAK*), a tool used to move container images; and CRI-O (*https:// cri-o.io*), a container engine complaint with the Kubernetes container runtime interface for running applications.

Buildah supports the Dockerfile format, but its goal is to provide a lower-level interface to build container images without requiring a Dockerfile. Buildah is a daemonless solution that can create images inside a container without mounting the Docker socket. This functionality improves security and portability since it's easy to add Buildah builds on the fly to a CI/CD pipeline where the Linux or Kubernetes nodes do not require a Docker installation.

As we discussed, you can create a container image with or without a Dockerfile. Let's now create a simple HTTPD container image without a Dockerfile.

You can start from any base image such as CentOS:

```
buildah from centos
```

You should get output similar to this:

```
Resolved short name "centos" to a recorded short-name alias↳
  (origin: /etc/containers/registries.conf.d/shortnames.conf)
Getting image source signatures
Copying blob 926a85fb4806 done
Copying config 2f3766df23 done
Writing manifest to image destination
Storing signatures
centos-working-container
```

> Similarly to Docker and docker images, you can run the command buildah containers to get the list of available images from the container cache. If you also have installed Podman, this is similar to podman images.

In this case, the container image ID is centos-working-container, and you can refer to it for creating the other layers.

Now let's install the `httpd` package inside a new layer:

```
buildah run centos-working-container yum install httpd -y
```

You should get output similar to this:

```
CentOS Linux 8 - AppStream                    9.0 MB/s | 8.4 MB    00:00
CentOS Linux 8 - BaseOS                       436 kB/s | 4.6 MB    00:10
CentOS Linux 8 - Extras                        23 kB/s |  10 kB    00:00
Dependencies resolved.
================================================================================
 Package               Arch    Version                    Repository     Size
================================================================================
Installing:
 httpd                 x86_64  2.4.37-43.module_el8.5.0+1022+b541f3b1
Installing dependencies:
 apr                   x86_64  1.6.3-12.el8
 apr-util              x86_64  1.6.1-6.el8
 brotli                x86_64  1.0.6-3.el8
 centos-logos-httpd    noarch  85.8-2.el8
 httpd-filesystem      noarch  2.4.37-43.module_el8.5.0+1022+b541f3b1
 httpd-tools           x86_64  2.4.37-43.module_el8.5.0+1022+b541f3b1
 mailcap               noarch  2.1.48-3.el8
 mod_http2             x86_64  1.15.7-3.module_el8.4.0+778+c970deab
Installing weak dependencies:
 apr-util-bdb          x86_64  1.6.1-6.el8
 apr-util-openssl      x86_64  1.6.1-6.el8
Enabling module streams:
...
Complete!
```

Now let's copy a welcome HTML page inside the container running HTTPD. You can find the source code in this book's repo (*https://oreil.ly/azx91*):

```
<html>
    <head>
        <title>GitOps CookBook example</title>
    </head>
    <body>
        <h1>Hello, World!</h1>
    </body>
</html>
```

```
buildah copy centos-working-container index.html /var/www/html/index.html
```

For each new layer added, you should get output with the new container image hash, similar to the following:

```
78c6e1dcd6f819581b54094fd38a3fd8f170a2cb768101e533c964e04aacab2e
```

```
buildah config --entrypoint "/usr/sbin/httpd -DFOREGROUND" centos-working-container
```

```
buildah commit centos-working-container quay.io/gitops-cookbook/gitops-website
```

You should get output similar to this:

```
Getting image source signatures
Copying blob 618ce6bf40a6 skipped: already exists
Copying blob eb8c13ba832f done
Copying config b825e91208 done
Writing manifest to image destination
Storing signatures
b825e91208c33371e209cc327abe4f53ee501d5679c127cd71c4d10cd03e5370
```

Your container image is now in the container cache, ready to run or push to another registry.

As mentioned before, Buildah can also create container images from a Dockerfile. Let's make the same container image from the Dockerfile listed here:

```
FROM centos:latest
RUN yum -y install httpd
COPY index.html /var/www/html/index.html
EXPOSE 80
CMD ["/usr/sbin/httpd", "-DFOREGROUND"]

buildah bud -f Dockerfile -t quay.io/gitops-cookbook/gitops-website

STEP 1: FROM centos:latest
Resolved short name "centos" to a recorded short-name alias↵
 (origin: /etc/containers/registries.conf.d/shortnames.conf)
Getting image source signatures
Copying blob 926a85fb4806 done
Copying config 2f3766df23 done
Writing manifest to image destination
Storing signatures
STEP 2: RUN yum -y install httpd
CentOS Linux 8 - AppStream          9.6 MB/s | 8.4 MB    00:00
CentOS Linux 8 - BaseOS             7.5 MB/s | 4.6 MB    00:00
CentOS Linux 8 - Extras              63 kB/s |  10 kB    00:00
Dependencies resolved.
...
Complete!
STEP 3: COPY index.html /var/www/html/index.html
STEP 4: EXPOSE 80
STEP 5: CMD ["/usr/sbin/httpd", "-DFOREGROUND"]
STEP 6: COMMIT quay.io/gitops-cookbook/gitops-website
Getting image source signatures
Copying blob 618ce6bf40a6 skipped: already exists
Copying blob 1be523a47735 done
Copying config 3128caf147 done
Writing manifest to image destination
Storing signatures
--> 3128caf1475
3128caf147547e43b84c13c241585d23a32601f2c2db80b966185b03cb6a8025
```

If you have also installed Podman, you can run it this way:

```
podman run -p 8080:80 -ti quay.io/gitops-cookbook/gitops-website
```

Then you can test it by opening the browser on *http://localhost:8080*.

Discussion

With Buildah, you have the opportunity to create container images from scratch or starting from a Dockerfile. You don't need to install Docker, and everything is designed around security: rootless mechanism, daemonless utilities, and more refined control of creating image layers.

Buildah can also build images from scratch, thus it creates an empty layer similar to the `FROM scratch` Dockerfile statement. This aspect is useful for creating very lightweight images containing only the packages needed to run your application, as you can see in Figure 3-2.

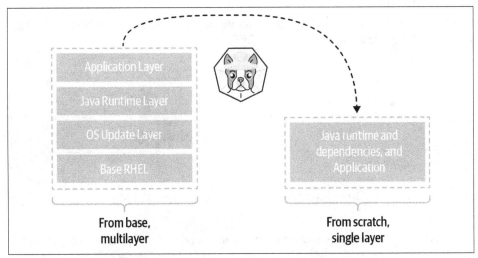

Figure 3-2. Buildah image shrink

A good example use case for a scratch build is considering the development images versus staging or production images. During development, container images may require a compiler and other tools. However, in production, you may only need the runtime or your packages.

See Also

- Running Buildah inside a container (*https://oreil.ly/GUfss*)

3.4 Building a Container with Buildpacks

Problem

Creating container image by using Dockerfiles can be challenging at scale. You want a tool complementing Docker that can inspect your application source code to create container images without writing a Dockerfile.

Solution

Cloud Native Buildpacks (*https://oreil.ly/psc6h*) is an open source project that provides a set of executables to inspect your app source code and to create a plan to build and run your application.

Buildpacks can create OCI-compliant container images without a Dockerfile, starting from the app source code, as you can see in Figure 3-3.

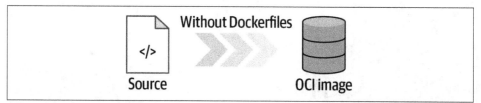

Figure 3-3. Buildpacks builds

This mechanism consists of two phases:

Detection
> Buildpacks tooling will navigate your source code to discover which programming language or framework is used (e.g., POM, NPM files, Python requirements, etc.) and assign a suitable buildpack for the build.

Building
> Once a buildpack is found, the source is compiled and Buildpacks creates a container image with the appropriate entry point and startup scripts.

To use Buildpacks, you have to download the pack (*https://oreil.ly/K0gGM*) CLI for your operating system (Mac, Windows, Linux), and also have Docker installed.

> On macOS, pack is available through Homebrew (*https://brew.sh*) as follows:
>
> ```
> brew install buildpacks/tap/pack
> ```

Now let's start creating our container image with Buildpacks from a sample Node.js app. You can find the app source code in this book's repository (*https://oreil.ly/eViRN*):

```
cd chapters/ch03/nodejs-app
```

The app directory structure contains a *package.json* file, a manifest listing Node.js packages required for this build, which helps Buildpacks understand which buildpack to use.

You can verify it with this command:

```
pack builder suggest
```

You should get output similar to this:

```
Suggested builders:
        Google:                 gcr.io/buildpacks/builder:v1↳
                Ubuntu 18 base image with buildpacks for .NET, Go, Java, Node.js,↳
                and Python
        Heroku:                 heroku/buildpacks:18↳
                Base builder for Heroku-18 stack, based on ubuntu:18.04 base↳
                image
        Heroku:                 heroku/buildpacks:20↳
                Base builder for Heroku-20 stack, based on ubuntu:20.04 base↳
                image
        Paketo Buildpacks:      paketobuildpacks/builder:base↳
                Ubuntu bionic base image with buildpacks for Java, .NET Core,↳
                Node.js, Go, Python, Ruby, NGINX and Procfile
        Paketo Buildpacks:      paketobuildpacks/builder:full↳
                Ubuntu bionic base image with buildpacks for Java, .NET Core,↳
                Node.js, Go, Python, PHP, Ruby, Apache HTTPD, NGINX and Procfile
        Paketo Buildpacks:      paketobuildpacks/builder:tiny↳
                Tiny base image (bionic build image, distroless-like run image)↳
                with buildpacks for Java, Java Native Image and Go
```

Now you can decide to pick one of the suggested buildpacks. Let's try the paketo buildpacks/builder:base, which also contains the Node.js runtime:

```
pack build nodejs-app --builder paketobuildpacks/builder:base
```

 Run pack builder inspect paketobuildpacks/builder:base to know the exact content of libraries and frameworks available in this buildpack.

The building process should start accordingly, and after a while, it should finish, and you should get output similar to this:

```
base: Pulling from paketobuildpacks/builder
bf99a8b93828: Pulling fs layer
...
```

```
Digest: sha256:7034e52388c11c5f7ee7ae8f2d7d794ba427cc2802f687dd9650d96a70ac0772
Status: Downloaded newer image for paketobuildpacks/builder:base
base-cnb: Pulling from paketobuildpacks/run
bf99a8b93828: Already exists
9d58a4841c3f: Pull complete
77a4f59032ac: Pull complete
24e58505e5e0: Pull complete
Digest: sha256:59aa1da9db6d979e21721e306b9ce99a7c4e3d1663c4c20f74f9b3876cce5192
Status: Downloaded newer image for paketobuildpacks/run:base-cnb
===> ANALYZING
Previous image with name "nodejs-app" not found
===> DETECTING
5 of 10 buildpacks participating
paketo-buildpacks/ca-certificates 3.0.1
paketo-buildpacks/node-engine     0.11.2
paketo-buildpacks/npm-install     0.6.2
paketo-buildpacks/node-module-bom 0.2.0
paketo-buildpacks/npm-start       0.6.1
===> RESTORING
===> BUILDING
...
Paketo NPM Start Buildpack 0.6.1
  Assigning launch processes
    web: node server.js

===> EXPORTING
Adding layer 'paketo-buildpacks/ca-certificates:helper'
Adding layer 'paketo-buildpacks/node-engine:node'
Adding layer 'paketo-buildpacks/npm-install:modules'
Adding layer 'launch.sbom'
Adding 1/1 app layer(s)
Adding layer 'launcher'
Adding layer 'config'
Adding layer 'process-types'
Adding label 'io.buildpacks.lifecycle.metadata'
Adding label 'io.buildpacks.build.metadata'
Adding label 'io.buildpacks.project.metadata'
Setting default process type 'web'
Saving nodejs-app...
*** Images (82b805699d6b):
      nodejs-app
Adding cache layer 'paketo-buildpacks/node-engine:node'
Adding cache layer 'paketo-buildpacks/npm-install:modules'
Adding cache layer 'paketo-buildpacks/node-module-bom:cyclonedx-node-module'
Successfully built image nodejs-app
```

Now let's run it with Docker:

```
docker run --rm -p 3000:3000 nodejs-app
```

You should get output similar to this:

```
Server running at http://0.0.0.0:3000/
```

View the running application:

```
curl http://localhost:3000/
```

You should get output similar to this:

```
Hello Buildpacks!
```

Discussion

Cloud Native Buildpacks is an incubating project in the Cloud Native Computing Foundation (CNCF), and it supports both Docker and Kubernetes. On Kubernetes, it can be used with Tekton (*https://tekton.dev*), a Kubernetes-native CI/CD system that can run Buildpacks as a Tekton Task to create container images. It recently adopted the Boson Project (*https://oreil.ly/F0OTs*) to provide a functions-as-a-service (FaaS) experience on Kubernetes with Knative, by enabling the build of functions via buildpacks.

See Also

- Using Buildpacks with Tekton Pipelines (*https://oreil.ly/wFIHd*)
- FaaS Knative Boson project's buildpacks (*https://oreil.ly/p1U6n*)

3.5 Building a Container Using Shipwright and kaniko in Kubernetes

Problem

You need to create a container image, and you want to do it with Kubernetes.

Solution

Kubernetes is well known as a container orchestration platform to deploy and manage apps. However, it doesn't include support for building container images out-of-the-box. Indeed, according to Kubernetes documentation (*https://oreil.ly/qgpKi*): "(Kubernetes) Does not deploy source code and does not build your application. Continuous Integration, Delivery, and Deployment (CI/CD) workflows are determined by organization cultures and preferences as well as technical requirements."

As mentioned, one standard option is to rely on CI/CD systems for this purpose, like Tekton (see Chapter 6). Another option is to use a framework to manage builds with many underlying tools, such as the one we discussed in the previous recipes. One example is Shipwright.

Shipwright (*https://shipwright.io*) is an extensible framework for building container images on Kubernetes. It supports popular tools such as Buildah, Cloud Native Buildpacks, and kaniko. It uses Kubernetes-style APIs, and it runs workloads using Tekton.

The benefit for developers is a simplified approach for building container images, by defining a minimal YAML file that does not require any previous knowledge of containers or container engines. This approach makes this solution agnostic and highly integrated with the Kubernetes API ecosystem.

The first thing to do is to install Shipwright to your Kubernetes cluster, say kind or Minikube (see Chapter 2), following the documentation (*https://oreil.ly/FWvXv*) or from OperatorHub.io (*https://oreil.ly/6Ds5R*).

 Using Operators and Operator Lifecycle Manager (OLM) gives consistency for installing/uninstalling software on Kubernetes, along with dependency management and lifecycle control. For instance, the Tekton Operator dependency is automatically resolved and installed if you install Shipwright via the Operator. Check the OLM documentation (*https://oreil.ly/V3k2p*) for details with this approach.

Let's follow the standard procedure from the documentation. First you need to install the Tekton dependency. At the time of writing this book, it is version 0.30.0:

```
kubectl apply -f \
    https://storage.googleapis.com/tekton-releases/pipeline/previous/v0.30.0/
release.yaml
```

Then you install Shipwright. At the time of writing this book, it is version 0.7.0:

```
kubectl apply -f \
    https://github.com/shipwright-io/build/releases/download/v0.7.0/release.yaml
```

Finally, you install Shipwright build strategies:

```
kubectl apply -f \
    https://github.com/shipwright-io/build/releases/download/v0.7.0/sample-
strategies.yaml
```

Once you have installed Shipwright, you can start creating your container image build using one of these tools:

- kaniko
- Cloud Native Buildpacks
- BuildKit
- Buildah

Let's explore kaniko.

kaniko (*https://oreil.ly/ncdWg*) is another dockerless solution to build container images from a Dockerfile inside a container or Kubernetes cluster. Shipwright brings additional APIs to Kubernetes to use tools such as kaniko to create container images, acting as an abstract layer that can be considered an extensible building system for Kubernetes.

Let's explore the APIs that are defined from Cluster Resource Definitions (CRDs):

ClusterBuildStrategy
: Represents the type of build to execute.

Build
: Represents the build. It includes the specification of one ClusterBuildStrategy object.

BuildRun
: Represents a running build. The build starts when this object is created.

Run the following command to check all available ClusterBuildStrategy (CBS) objects:

```
kubectl get cbs
```

You should get a list of available CBSs to consume:

```
NAME                      AGE
buildah                   26s
buildkit                  26s
buildpacks-v3             26s
buildpacks-v3-heroku      26s
kaniko                    26s
kaniko-trivy              26s
ko                        26s
source-to-image           26s
source-to-image-redhat    26s
```

 This CRD is cluster-wide, available for all namespaces. If you don't see any items, please install the Shipwright build strategies as discussed previously.

Shipwright will generate a container image on the Kubernetes nodes container cache, and then it can push it to a container registry.

You need to provide the credentials to push the image to the registry in the form of a Kubernetes Secret. For example, if you use Quay you can create one like the following:

```
REGISTRY_SERVER=quay.io
REGISTRY_USER=<your_registry_user>
REGISTRY_PASSWORD=<your_registry_password>
EMAIL=<your_email>
kubectl create secret docker-registry push-secret \
    --docker-server=$REGISTRY_SERVER \
    --docker-username=$REGISTRY_USER \
    --docker-password=$REGISTRY_PASSWORD  \
    --docker-email=$EMAIL
```

 With Quay, you can use an encrypted password instead of using your account password. See the documentation for more details.

Now let's create a *build-kaniko.yaml* file containing the Build object that will use kaniko to containerize a Node.js sample app. You can find the source code in this book's repository (*https://oreil.ly/S84zu*):

```
apiVersion: shipwright.io/v1alpha1
kind: Build
metadata:
  name: buildpack-nodejs-build
spec:
  source:
    url: https://github.com/shipwright-io/sample-nodejs ❶
    contextDir: docker-build ❷
  strategy:
    name: kaniko ❸
    kind: ClusterBuildStrategy
  output:
    image: quay.io/gitops-cookbook/sample-nodejs:latest ❹
    credentials:
      name: push-secret ❺
```

❶ Repository to grab the source code from.

❷ The directory where the source code is present.

❸ The ClusterBuildStrategy to use.

❹ The destination of the resulting container image. Change this with your container registry repo.

❺ The secret to use to authenticate to the container registry and push the image.

Now, let's create the `Build` object:

```
kubectl create -f build-kaniko.yaml
```

You should get output similar to this:

```
build.shipwright.io/kaniko-nodejs-build created
```

Let's list the available builds:

```
kubectl get builds
```

You should get output similar to the following:

```
NAME                    REGISTERED   REASON      BUILDSTRATEGYKIND↵
     BUILDSTRATEGYNAME   CREATIONTIME
kaniko-nodejs-build     True         Succeeded   ClusterBuildStrategy↵
     kaniko              13s
```

At this point, your `Build` is `REGISTERED`, but it's not started yet. Let's create the following object in order to start it:

```
apiVersion: shipwright.io/v1alpha1
kind: BuildRun
metadata:
  generateName: kaniko-nodejs-buildrun-
spec:
  buildRef:
    name: kaniko-nodejs-build
```

```
kubectl create -f buildrun.yaml
```

If you check the list of running pods, you should see one being created:

```
kubectl get pods
```

```
NAME                                               READY   STATUS          RESTARTS↵
     AGE
kaniko-nodejs-buildrun-b9mmb-qbrgl-pod-dk7xt   0/3     PodInitializing   0↵
     19s
```

When the `STATUS` changes, the build will start, and you can track the progress by checking the logs from the containers used by this pod to run the build in multiple steps:

step-source-default
> The first step, used to get the source code

step-build-and-push
> The step to run the build, either from source code or from a Dockerfile like in this case with kaniko

step-results
> The result of the build

Let's check the logs of the building phase:

```
kubectl logs -f kaniko-nodejs-buildrun-b9mmb-qbrgl-pod-dk7xt -c step-build-and-push

INFO[0001] Retrieving image manifest ghcr.io/shipwright-io/shipwright-samples/
node:12
INFO[0001] Retrieving image ghcr.io/shipwright-io/shipwright-samples/node:12↳
 from registry ghcr.io
INFO[0002] Built cross stage deps: map[]
INFO[0002] Retrieving image manifest ghcr.io/shipwright-io/shipwright-samples/
node:12
INFO[0002] Returning cached image manifest
INFO[0002] Executing 0 build triggers
INFO[0002] Unpacking rootfs as cmd COPY . /app requires it.
INFO[0042] COPY . /app
INFO[0042] Taking snapshot of files...
INFO[0042] WORKDIR /app
INFO[0042] cmd: workdir
INFO[0042] Changed working directory to /app
INFO[0042] No files changed in this command, skipping snapshotting.
INFO[0042] RUN     pwd &&     ls -l &&     npm install &&↳
    npm run print-http-server-version
INFO[0042] Taking snapshot of full filesystem...
INFO[0052] cmd: /bin/sh
INFO[0052] args: [-c pwd &&     ls -l &&     npm install &&↳
    npm run print-http-server-version]
INFO[0052] Running: [/bin/sh -c pwd &&     ls -l &&     npm install &&↳
    npm run print-http-server-version]
/app
total 44
-rw-r--r-- 1 node node   261 Jan 27 14:29 Dockerfile
-rw-r--r-- 1 node node 30000 Jan 27 14:29 package-lock.json
-rw-r--r-- 1 node node   267 Jan 27 14:29 package.json
drwxr-xr-x 2 node node  4096 Jan 27 14:29 public
npm WARN npm-simple-renamed@0.0.1 No repository field.
npm WARN npm-simple-renamed@0.0.1 No license field.

added 90 packages from 40 contributors and audited 90 packages in 6.405s

10 packages are looking for funding
    run `npm fund` for details

found 0 vulnerabilities


> npm-simple-renamed@0.0.1 print-http-server-version /app
> serve -v

13.0.2
INFO[0060] Taking snapshot of full filesystem...
INFO[0062] EXPOSE 8080
INFO[0062] cmd: EXPOSE
INFO[0062] Adding exposed port: 8080/tcp
INFO[0062] CMD ["npm", "start"]
```

```
INFO[0070] Pushing image to quay.io/gitops-cookbook/sample-nodejs:latest
INFO[0393] Pushed image to 1 destinations
```

The image is built and pushed to the registry, and you can check the result from this command as well:

```
kubectl get buildruns
```

And on your registry, as shown in Figure 3-4.

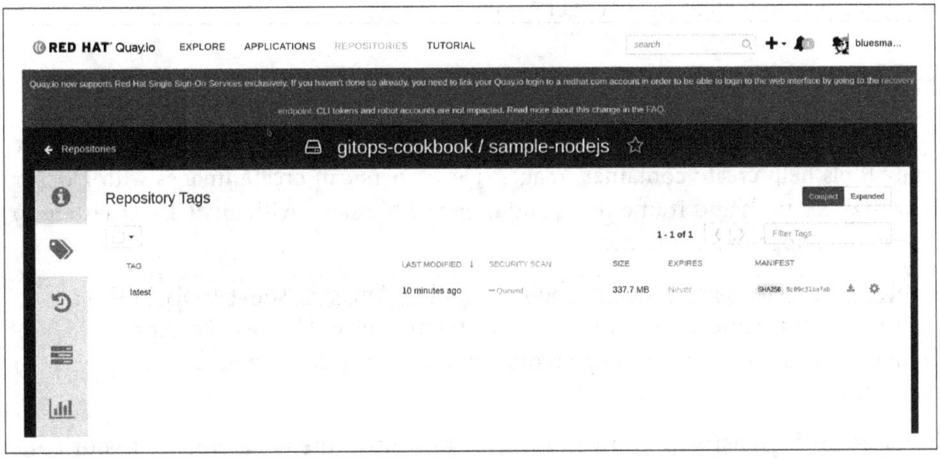

Figure 3-4. Image pushed to Quay

Discussion

Shipwright provides a convenient way to create container images on Kubernetes, and its agnostic approach makes it robust and interoperable. The project aims at being the Build API for Kubernetes, providing an easier path for developers to automate on Kubernetes. As Tekton runs under the hood creating builds, Shipwright also makes transitioning from micropipeline to extended pipeline workflows on Kubernetes easier.

As a reference, if you would like to create a build with Buildah instead of kaniko, it's just a ClusterBuildStrategy change in your Build object:

```
apiVersion: shipwright.io/v1alpha1
kind: Build
metadata:
  name: buildpack-nodejs-build
spec:
  source:
    url: https://github.com/shipwright-io/sample-nodejs
    contextDir: source-build ❶
  strategy:
    name: buildah ❷
    kind: ClusterBuildStrategy
```

```
output:
  image: quay.io/gitops-cookbook/sample-nodejs:latest
  credentials:
    name: push-secret
```

 As we discussed previously in Recipe 3.3, Buildah can create the container image from the source code. It doesn't need a Dockerfile.

❷ Selecting Buildah as the `ClusterBuildStrategy`.

3.6 Final Thoughts

The container format is the de facto standard for packaging applications, and today many tools help create container images. Developers can create images with Docker or with other tools and frameworks and then use the same with any CI/CD system to deploy their apps to Kubernetes.

While Kubernetes per se doesn't build container images, some tools interact with the Kubernetes API ecosystem to add this functionality. This aspect improves development velocity and consistency across environments, delegating this complexity to the platform.

In the following chapters, you will see how to control the deployment of your containers running on Kubernetes with tools such as Kustomize or Helm, and then how to add automation to support highly scalable workloads with CI/CD and GitOps.

## CHAPTER 4

Kustomize

Deploying to a Kubernetes cluster is, in summary, applying some YAML files and checking the result.

The hard part is developing the initial YAML files version; after that, usually, they suffer only small changes such as updating the container image tag version, the number of replicas, or a new configuration value. One option is to make these changes directly in the YAML files—it works, but any error in this version (modification of the wrong line, deleting something by mistake, putting in the wrong whitespace) might be catastrophic.

For this reason, some tools let you define base Kubernetes manifests (which change infrequently) and specific files (maybe one for each environment) for setting the parameters that change more frequently. One of these tools is Kustomize.

In this chapter, you'll learn how to use Kustomize to manage Kubernetes resource files in a template-free way without using any DSL.

The first step is to create a Kustomize project and deploy it to a Kubernetes cluster (see Recipe 4.1).

After the first deployment, the application is automatically updated with a new container image, a new configuration value, or any other field, such as the replica number (see Recipes 4.2 and 4.3).

If you've got several running environments (i.e., staging, production, etc.), you need to manage them similarly. Still, with its particularities, Kustomize lets you define a set of custom values per environment (see Recipe 4.4).

Application configuration values are properties usually mapped as a Kubernetes `ConfigMap`. Any change (and its consequent update on the cluster) on a `ConfigMap` doesn't trigger a rolling update of the application, which means that the application will run with the previous version until you manually restart it.

Kustomize provides some functions to automatically execute a rolling update when the ConfigMap of an application changes (see Recipe 4.5).

4.1 Using Kustomize to Deploy Kubernetes Resources

Problem

You want to deploy several Kubernetes resources at once.

Solution

Use Kustomize (*https://kustomize.io*) to configure which resources to deploy.

Deploying an application to a Kubernetes cluster isn't as trivial as just applying one YAML/JSON file containing a Kubernetes Deployment object. Usually, other Kubernetes objects must be defined like Service, Ingress, ConfigMaps, etc., which makes things a bit more complicated in terms of managing and updating these resources (the more resources to maintain, the more chance to update the wrong one) as well as applying them to a cluster (should we run multiple kubectl commands?).

Kustomize is a CLI tool, integrated within the kubectl tool to manage, customize, and apply Kubernetes resources in a *template-less* way.

With Kustomize, you need to set a base directory with standard Kubernetes resource files (no placeholders are required) and create a *kustomization.yaml* file where resources and customizations are declared, as you can see in Figure 4-1.

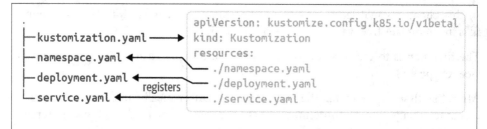

Figure 4-1. Kustomize layout

Let's deploy a simple web page with HTML, JavaScript, and CSS files.

First, open a terminal window and create a directory named *pacman*, then create three Kubernetes resource files to create a Namespace, a Deployment, and a Service with the following content.

The namespace at *pacman/namespace.yaml*:

```yaml
apiVersion: v1
kind: Namespace
metadata:
  name: pacman
```

The deployment file at *pacman/deployment.yaml*:

```yaml
apiVersion: apps/v1
kind: Deployment
metadata:
  name: pacman-kikd
  namespace: pacman
  labels:
    app.kubernetes.io/name: pacman-kikd
spec:
  replicas: 1
  selector:
    matchLabels:
      app.kubernetes.io/name: pacman-kikd
  template:
    metadata:
      labels:
        app.kubernetes.io/name: pacman-kikd
    spec:
      containers:
        - image: lordofthejars/pacman-kikd:1.0.0
          imagePullPolicy: Always
          name: pacman-kikd
          ports:
            - containerPort: 8080
              name: http
              protocol: TCP
```

The service file at *pacman/service.yaml*:

```yaml
apiVersion: v1
kind: Service
metadata:
  labels:
    app.kubernetes.io/name: pacman-kikd
  name: pacman-kikd
  namespace: pacman
spec:
  ports:
    - name: http
      port: 8080
      targetPort: 8080
  selector:
    app.kubernetes.io/name: pacman-kikd
```

Notice that these files are Kubernetes files that you could apply to a Kubernetes cluster without any problem as no special characters or placeholders are used.

The second thing is to create the *kustomization.yaml* file in the *pacman* directory containing the list of resources that belongs to the application and are applied when running Kustomize:

```
apiVersion: kustomize.config.k8s.io/v1beta1
kind: Kustomization ❶
resources: ❷
- ./namespace.yaml
- ./deployment.yaml
- ./service.yaml
```

❶ Kustomization file

❷ Resources belonging to the application processed in depth-first order

At this point, we can apply the kustomization file into a running cluster by running the following command:

```
kubectl apply --dry-run=client -o yaml \ ❶
        -k ./ ❷ ❸
```

❶ Prints the result of the kustomization run, without sending the result to the cluster

❷ With -k option sets kubectl to use the kustomization file

❸ Directory with parent *kustomization.yaml* file

 We assume you've already started a *Minikube* cluster as shown in Recipe 2.3.

The output is the YAML file that would be sent to the server if the dry-run option was not used:

```
apiVersion: v1
items: ❶
- apiVersion: v1
  kind: Namespace ❷
  metadata:
    name: pacman
- apiVersion: v1
  kind: Service ❸
  metadata:
    labels:
      app.kubernetes.io/name: pacman-kikd
    name: pacman-kikd
    namespace: pacman
```

```
  spec:
    ports:
    - name: http
      port: 8080
      targetPort: 8080
    selector:
      app.kubernetes.io/name: pacman-kikd
- apiVersion: apps/v1
  kind: Deployment  ❹
  metadata:
    labels:
      app.kubernetes.io/name: pacman-kikd
    name: pacman-kikd
    namespace: pacman
  spec:
    replicas: 1
    selector:
      matchLabels:
        app.kubernetes.io/name: pacman-kikd
    template:
      metadata:
        labels:
          app.kubernetes.io/name: pacman-kikd
      spec:
        containers:
        - image: lordofthejars/pacman-kikd:1.0.0
          imagePullPolicy: Always
          name: pacman-kikd
          ports:
          - containerPort: 8080
            name: http
            protocol: TCP
kind: List
metadata: {}
```

❶ List of all Kubernetes objects defined in *kustomization.yaml* to apply

❷ The namespace document

❸ The service document

❹ The deployment document

Discussion

The resources section supports different inputs in addition to directly setting the YAML files.

For example, you can set a base directory with its own *kustomization.yaml* and Kubernetes resources files and refer it from another *kustomization.yaml* file placed in another directory.

Given the following directory layout:

```
.
├── base
│   ├── kustomization.yaml
│   └── deployment.yaml
├── kustomization.yaml
├── configmap.yaml
```

And the Kustomization definitions in the *base* directory:

```
apiVersion: kustomize.config.k8s.io/v1beta1
kind: Kustomization
resources:
- ./deployment.yaml
```

You'll see that the root directory has a link to the *base* directory and a `ConfigMap` definition:

```
apiVersion: kustomize.config.k8s.io/v1beta1
kind: Kustomization
resources:
- ./base
- ./configmap.yaml
```

So, applying the root kustomization file will automatically apply the resources defined in the base kustomization file.

Also, `resources` can reference external assets from a URL following the HashiCorp URL (*https://oreil.ly/lbeQC*) format. For example, we refer to a GitHub repository by setting the URL:

```
resources:
- github.com/lordofthejars/mysql ❶
- github.com/lordofthejars/mysql?ref=test ❷
```

❶ Repository with a root-level *kustomization.yaml* file

❷ Repository with a root-level *kustomization.yaml* file on branch test

You've seen the application of a Kustomize file using `kubectl`, but Kustomize also comes with its own CLI tool offering a set of commands to interact with Kustomize resources.

The equivalent command to build Kustomize resources using `kustomize` instead of `kubectl` is:

```
kustomize build
```

And the output is:

```
apiVersion: v1
kind: Namespace
metadata:
  name: pacman
---
apiVersion: v1
kind: Service
metadata:
  labels:
    app.kubernetes.io/name: pacman-kikd
  name: pacman-kikd
  namespace: pacman
spec:
  ports:
  - name: http
    port: 8080
    targetPort: 8080
  selector:
    app.kubernetes.io/name: pacman-kikd
---
apiVersion: apps/v1
kind: Deployment
metadata:
  labels:
    app.kubernetes.io/name: pacman-kikd
  name: pacman-kikd
  namespace: pacman
spec:
  replicas: 1
  selector:
    matchLabels:
      app.kubernetes.io/name: pacman-kikd
  template:
    metadata:
      labels:
        app.kubernetes.io/name: pacman-kikd
    spec:
      containers:
      - image: lordofthejars/pacman-kikd:1.0.0
        imagePullPolicy: Always
        name: pacman-kikd
        ports:
        - containerPort: 8080
          name: http
          protocol: TCP
```

If you want to apply this output generated by `kustomize` to the cluster, run the following command:

```
kustomize build . | kubectl apply -f -
```

See Also

- Kustomize (*https://kustomize.io*)
- kustomize/v4.4.1 on GitHub (*https://oreil.ly/h2yNd*)
- HashiCorp URL format (*https://oreil.ly/n7jwr*)

4.2 Updating the Container Image in Kustomize

Problem

You want to update the container image from a deployment file using Kustomize.

Solution

Use the `images` section to update the container image.

One of the most important and most-used operations in software development is updating the application to a newer version either with a bug fix or with a new feature. In Kubernetes, this means that you need to create a new container image, and name it accordingly using the `tag` section (`<registry>/<username>/<project>:<tag>`).

Given the following partial deployment file:

```
spec:
    containers:
        - image: lordofthejars/pacman-kikd:1.0.0 ❶
          imagePullPolicy: Always
          name: pacman-kikd
```

❶ Service 1.0.0 is deployed

We can update the version tag to 1.0.1 by using the `images` section in the *kustomization.yaml* file:

```
apiVersion: kustomize.config.k8s.io/v1beta1
kind: Kustomization
resources:
- ./namespace.yaml
- ./deployment.yaml
- ./service.yaml
images: ❶
- name: lordofthejars/pacman-kikd ❷
  newTag: 1.0.1 ❸
```

1 `images` section

2 Sets the name of the image to *update*

3 Sets the new tag value for the image

Finally, use `kubectl` in `dry-run` or `kustomize` to validate that the output of the deployment file contains the new tag version. In a terminal window, run the following command:

```
kustomize build
```

The output of the preceding command is:

```
...
apiVersion: apps/v1
kind: Deployment
metadata:
  labels:
    app.kubernetes.io/name: pacman-kikd
  name: pacman-kikd
  namespace: pacman
spec:
  replicas: 1
  selector:
    matchLabels:
      app.kubernetes.io/name: pacman-kikd
  template:
    metadata:
      labels:
        app.kubernetes.io/name: pacman-kikd
    spec:
      containers:
      - image: lordofthejars/pacman-kikd:1.0.1  1
        imagePullPolicy: Always
        name: pacman-kikd
        ports:
        - containerPort: 8080
          name: http
          protocol: TCP
```

1 Version set in the `kustomize.yaml` file

Kustomize is not intrusive, which means that the original *deployment.yaml* file still contains the original tag (`1.0.0`).

Discussion

One way to update the `newTag` field is by editing the *kustomization.yaml* file, but you can also use the `kustomize` tool for this purpose.

Run the following command in the same directory as the *kustomization.yaml* file:

```
kustomize edit set image lordofthejars/pacman-kikd:1.0.2
```

Check the content of the *kustomization.yaml* file to see that the `newTag` field has been updated:

```
...
images:
- name: lordofthejars/pacman-kikd
  newTag: 1.0.2
```

4.3 Updating Any Kubernetes Field in Kustomize

Problem

You want to update a field (i.e., number of replicas) using Kustomize.

Solution

Use the `patches` section to specify a change using the JSON Patch specification.

In the previous recipe, you saw how to update the container image tag, but sometimes you might change other parameters like the number of replicas or add annotations, labels, limits, etc.

To cover these scenarios, Kustomize supports the use of JSON Patch to modify any Kubernetes resource defined as a Kustomize resource. To use it, you need to specify the JSON Patch expression to apply and which resource to apply the patch to.

For example, we can modify the number of replicas in the following partial deployment file from one to three:

```
apiVersion: apps/v1
kind: Deployment
metadata:
  name: pacman-kikd
  namespace: pacman
  labels:
    app.kubernetes.io/name: pacman-kikd
spec:
  replicas: 1
  selector:
    matchLabels:
      app.kubernetes.io/name: pacman-kikd
  template:
```

```
  metadata:
    labels:
      app.kubernetes.io/name: pacman-kikd
  spec:
    containers:
...
```

First, let's update the *kustomization.yaml* file to modify the number of replicas defined in the deployment file:

```
apiVersion: kustomize.config.k8s.io/v1beta1
kind: Kustomization
resources:
- ./deployment.yaml
patches: ❶
  - target: ❷
      version: v1
      group: apps
      kind: Deployment
      name: pacman-kikd
      namespace: pacman
    patch: |- ❸
      - op: replace ❹
        path: /spec/replicas ❺
        value: 3 ❻
```

❶ Patch resource.

❷ `target` section sets which Kubernetes object needs to be changed. These values match the deployment file created previously.

❸ Patch expression.

❹ Modification of a value.

❺ Path to the field to modify.

❻ New value.

Finally, use kubectl in dry-run or kustomize to validate that the output of the deployment file contains the new tag version. In a terminal window, run the following command:

```
kustomize build
```

The output of the preceding command is:

```
apiVersion: apps/v1
kind: Deployment
metadata:
  labels:
    app.kubernetes.io/name: pacman-kikd
```

```
    name: pacman-kikd
    namespace: pacman
spec:
  replicas: 3
  selector:
    matchLabels:
      app.kubernetes.io/name: pacman-kikd
...
```

 The *replicas* value can also be updated using the `replicas` field in the *kustomization.yaml* file.

The equivalent Kustomize file using the `replicas` field is shown in the following snippet:

```
apiVersion: kustomize.config.k8s.io/v1beta1
kind: Kustomization
replicas:
- name: pacman-kikd ❶
  count: 3 ❷
resources:
- deployment.yaml
```

❶ Deployment to update the replicas

❷ New `replicas` value

Kustomize lets you add (or delete) values, in addition to modifying a value. Let's see how to add a new label:

```
...
patches:
  - target:
      version: v1
      group: apps
      kind: Deployment
      name: pacman-kikd
      namespace: pacman
    patch: |-
      - op: replace
        path: /spec/replicas
        value: 3
      - op: add ❶
        path: /metadata/labels/testkey ❷
        value: testvalue ❸
```

❶ Adds a new field with value

❷ Path with the field to add

❸ The value to set

The result of applying the file is:

```
apiVersion: apps/v1
kind: Deployment
metadata:
  labels:
    app.kubernetes.io/name: pacman-kikd
    testkey: testvalue ❶
  name: pacman-kikd
  namespace: pacman
spec:
  replicas: 3
  selector:
...
```

❶ Added label

Discussion

Instead of embedding a JSON Patch expression, you can create a YAML file with a Patch expression and refer to it using the `path` field instead of `patch`.

Create an external patch file named *external_patch* containing the JSON Patch expression:

```
- op: replace
  path: /spec/replicas
  value: 3
- op: add
  path: /metadata/labels/testkey
  value: testvalue
```

And change the `patch` field to `path` pointing to the patch file:

```
...
patches:
  - target:
      version: v1
      group: apps
      kind: Deployment
      name: pacman-kikd
      namespace: pacman
    path: external_patch.yaml ❶
```

❶ Path to external patch file

In addition to the JSON Patch expression, Kustomize also supports Strategic Merge Patch (*https://oreil.ly/vr3e3*) to modify Kubernetes resources. In summary, a Strategic Merge Patch (or *SMP*) is an incomplete YAML file that is merged against a completed YAML file.

Only a minimal deployment file with container name information is required to update a container image:

```
apiVersion: kustomize.config.k8s.io/v1beta1
kind: Kustomization
resources:
- ./deployment.yaml
patches:
  - target:
      labelSelector: "app.kubernetes.io/name=pacman-kikd" ❶
    patch: |- ❷
      apiVersion: apps/v1 ❸
      kind: Deployment
      metadata:
        name: pacman-kikd
      spec:
        template:
          spec:
            containers:
              - name: pacman-kikd
                image: lordofthejars/pacman-kikd:1.2.0 ❹
```

❶ Target is selected using label

❷ Patch is smart enough to detect if it is an SMP or JSON Patch

❸ This is a minimal deployment file

❹ Sets only the field to change, the rest is left as is

The generated output is the original *deployment.yaml* file but with the new container image:

```
apiVersion: apps/v1
kind: Deployment
metadata:
  labels:
    app.kubernetes.io/name: pacman-kikd
  name: pacman-kikd
  namespace: pacman
spec:
  replicas: 1
  selector:
    matchLabels:
      app.kubernetes.io/name: pacman-kikd
  template:
    metadata:
      labels:
        app.kubernetes.io/name: pacman-kikd
    spec:
      containers:
      - image: lordofthejars/pacman-kikd:1.2.0
```

```
    imagePullPolicy: Always
...
```

 path is supported as well.

See Also

- RFC 6902: JavaScript Object Notation (JSON) Patch (*https://oreil.ly/gDn1A*)
- Strategic Merge Patch (*https://oreil.ly/vr3e3*)

4.4 Deploying to Multiple Environments

Problem

You want to deploy the same application in different namespaces using Kustomize.

Solution

Use the `namespace` field to set the target namespace.

In some circumstances, it's good to have the application deployed in different name‐
spaces; for example, one namespace can be used as a *staging* environment, and
another one as the *production* namespace. In both cases, the base Kubernetes files are
the same, with minimal changes like the namespace deployed, some configuration
parameters, or container version, to mention a few. Figure 4-2 shows an example.

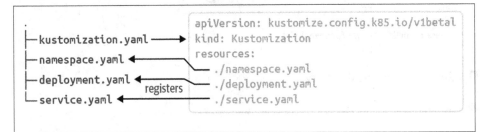

Figure 4-2. Kustomize layout

`kustomize` lets you define multiple changes with a different namespace, as overlays
on a common base using the `namespace` field. For this example, all base Kubernetes
resources are put in the `base` directory and a new directory is created for customiza‐
tions of each environment:

```
.
├── base ❶
│   ├── deployment.yaml
│   └── kustomization.yaml
├── production
│   └── kustomization.yaml ❷
└── staging
    └── kustomization.yaml ❸
```

❶ Base files

❷ Changes specific to production environment

❸ Changes specific to staging environment

The base kustomization file contains a reference to its resources:

```
apiVersion: kustomize.config.k8s.io/v1beta1
kind: Kustomization
resources:
- ./deployment.yaml
```

There is a kustomization file with some parameters set for each environment directory. These reference the *base* directory, the namespace to inject into Kubernetes
resources, and finally, the image to deploy, which in production is *1.1.0* but in staging
is *1.2.0-beta*.

For the staging environment, *kustomization.yaml* content is shown in the following
listing:

```
apiVersion: kustomize.config.k8s.io/v1beta1
kind: Kustomization
resources:
- ../base ❶
namespace: staging ❷
images:
- name: lordofthejars/pacman-kikd
  newTag: 1.2.0-beta ❸
```

❶ References to *base* directory

❷ Sets namespace to *staging*

❸ Sets the container tag for the *staging* environment

The kustomization file for production is similar to the staging one, but changes the
namespace and the tag:

```
apiVersion: kustomize.config.k8s.io/v1beta1
kind: Kustomization
resources:
- ../base
```

```
namespace: prod ❶
images:
- name: lordofthejars/pacman-kikd
  newTag: 1.1.0 ❷
```

❶   Sets namespace for *production*

❷   Sets the container tag for the *production* environment

Running `kustomize` produces different output depending on the directory where it is run; for example, running `kustomize build` in the *staging* directory produces:

```
apiVersion: apps/v1
kind: Deployment
metadata:
  labels:
    app.kubernetes.io/name: pacman-kikd
  name: pacman-kikd
  namespace: staging ❶
spec:
  replicas: 1
...
  template:
    metadata:
      labels:
        app.kubernetes.io/name: pacman-kikd
    spec:
      containers:
      - image: lordofthejars/pacman-kikd:1.2.0-beta ❷
...
```

❶   Namespace value is injected

❷   Container tag for the *staging* environment is injected

But if you run it in the *production* directory, the output is adapted to the production configuration:

```
apiVersion: apps/v1
kind: Deployment
metadata:
  labels:
    app.kubernetes.io/name: pacman-kikd
  name: pacman-kikd
  namespace: prod ❶
spec:
  replicas: 1
...
    spec:
      containers:
      - image: lordofthejars/pacman-kikd:1.1.0 ❷
...
```

❶ Injects the *production* namespace

❷ Container tag for the *production* environment

Discussion

Kustomize can preappend/append a value to the names of all resources and references. This is useful when a different name in the resource is required depending on the environment, or to set the version deployed in the name:

```
apiVersion: kustomize.config.k8s.io/v1beta1
kind: Kustomization
resources:
- ../base
namespace: staging
namePrefix: staging- ❶
nameSuffix: -v1-2-0 ❷
images:
- name: lordofthejars/pacman-kikd
  newTag: 1.2.0-beta
```

❶ Prefix to preappend

❷ Suffix to append

And the resulting output is as follows:

```
apiVersion: apps/v1
kind: Deployment
metadata:
  labels:
    app.kubernetes.io/name: pacman-kikd
  name: staging-pacman-kikd-v1-2-0 ❶
  namespace: staging
spec:
  ...
```

❶ New name of the deployment file

4.5 Generating ConfigMaps in Kustomize

Problem

You want to generate Kubernetes ConfigMaps using Kustomize.

Solution

Use the ConfigMapGenerator feature field to generate a Kubernetes ConfigMap resource on the fly.

Kustomize provides two ways of adding a `ConfigMap` as a Kustomize resource: either by declaring a `ConfigMap` as any other resource or declaring a `ConfigMap` from a `ConfigMapGenerator`.

While using `ConfigMap` as a resource offers no other advantage than populating Kubernetes resources as any other resource, `ConfigMapGenerator` automatically appends a hash to the `ConfigMap` metadata name and also modifies the deployment file with the new hash. This minimal change has a deep impact on the application's lifecycle, as we'll see soon in the example.

Let's consider an application running in Kubernetes and configured using a `Config Map`—for example, a database timeout connection parameter. We decided to increase this number at some point, so the `ConfigMap` file is changed to this new value, and we deploy the application again. Since the `ConfigMap` is the only changed file, no rolling update of the application is done. A manual rolling update of the application needs to be triggered to propagate the change to the application. Figure 4-3 shows what is changed when a `ConfigMap` object is updated.

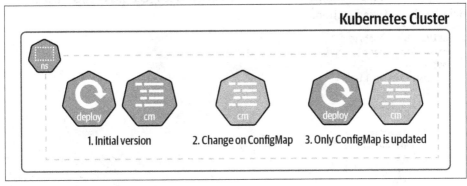

Figure 4-3. Change of a `ConfigMap`

But, if `ConfigMapGenerator` manages the `ConfigMap`, any change on the configuration file also changes the deployment Kubernetes resource. Since the deployment file has changed too, an automatic rolling update is triggered when the resources are applied, as shown in Figure 4-4.

Moreover, when using `ConfigMapGenerator`, multiple configuration datafiles can be combined into a single `ConfigMap`, making a perfect use case when every environment has different configuration files.

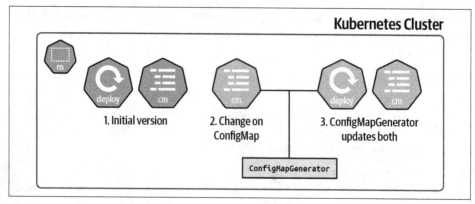

Figure 4-4. Change of a `ConfigMap` using `ConfigMapGenerator`

Let's start with a simple example, adding the `ConfigMapGenerator` section in the *kustomization.yaml* file.

The deployment file is similar to the one used in previous sections of this chapter but includes the `volumes` section:

```
apiVersion: apps/v1
kind: Deployment
metadata:
  name: pacman-kikd
spec:
  replicas: 1
  selector:
    matchLabels:
      app.kubernetes.io/name: pacman-kikd
  template:
    metadata:
      labels:
        app.kubernetes.io/name: pacman-kikd
    spec:
      containers:
      - image: lordofthejars/pacman-kikd:1.0.0
        imagePullPolicy: Always
        name: pacman-kikd
        volumeMounts:
        - name: config
          mountPath: /config
      volumes:
      - name: config
        configMap:
          name: pacman-configmap  ❶
```

❶ ConfigMap name is used in the *kustomization.yaml* file

The configuration properties are embedded within the *kustomization.yaml* file. Notice that the ConfigMap object is created on the fly when the kustomization file is built:

```
apiVersion: kustomize.config.k8s.io/v1beta1
kind: Kustomization
resources:
- ./deployment.yaml
configMapGenerator:
- name: pacman-configmap ❶
  literals:      ❷
  - db-timeout=2000 ❸
  - db-username=Ada
```

❶   Name of the ConfigMap set in the deployment file

❷   Embeds configuration values in the file

❸   Sets a key/value pair for the properties

Finally, use kubectl in dry-run or kustomize to validate that the output of the deployment file contains the new tag version. In a terminal window, run the following command:

```
kustomize build
```

The output of the preceding command is a new ConfigMap with the configuration values set in *kustomization.yaml*. Moreover, the name of the ConfigMap is updated by appending a hash in both the generated ConfigMap and deployment:

```
apiVersion: v1
data: ❶
  db-timeout: "2000"
  db-username: Ada
kind: ConfigMap
metadata:
  name: pacman-configmap-96kb69b6t4 ❷
---
apiVersion: apps/v1
kind: Deployment
metadata:
  labels:
    app.kubernetes.io/name: pacman-kikd
  name: pacman-kikd
spec:
  replicas: 1
  selector:
    matchLabels:
      app.kubernetes.io/name: pacman-kikd
  template:
    metadata:
      labels:
```

```
      app.kubernetes.io/name: pacman-kikd
spec:
  containers:
  - image: lordofthejars/pacman-kikd:1.0.0
    imagePullPolicy: Always
    name: pacman-kikd
    volumeMounts:
    - mountPath: /config
      name: config
  volumes:
  - configMap:
      name: pacman-configmap-96kb69b6t4  ❸
    name: config
```

❶ ConfigMap with properties

❷ Name with hash

❸ Name field is updated to the one with the hash triggering a rolling update

Since the hash is calculated for any change in the configuration properties, a change on them provokes a change on the output triggering a rolling update of the application. Open the *kustomization.yaml* file and update the db-timeout literal from 2000 to 1000 and run kustomize build again. Notice the change in the ConfigMap name using a new hashed value:

```
apiVersion: v1
data:
  db-timeout: "1000"
  db-username: Ada
kind: ConfigMap
metadata:
  name: pacman-configmap-6952t58tb4  ❶
---
apiVersion: apps/v1
kind: Deployment
...
    volumes:
    - configMap:
        name: pacman-configmap-6952t58tb4
      name: config
```

❶ New hashed value

Discussion

ConfigMapGenerator also supports merging configuration properties from different sources.

Create a new *kustomization.yaml* file in the *dev_literals* directory, setting it as the previous directory and overriding the db-username value:

```
apiVersion: kustomize.config.k8s.io/v1beta1
kind: Kustomization
resources:
- ../literals ❶
configMapGenerator:
- name: pacman-configmap
  behavior: merge ❷
  literals:
  - db-username=Alexandra ❸
```

❶ Base directory

❷ Merge properties (can be create or replace too)

❸ Overridden value

Running the kustomize build command produces a ConfigMap containing a merge of both configuration properties:

```
apiVersion: v1
data:
  db-timeout: "1000" ❶
  db-username: Alexandra ❷
kind: ConfigMap
metadata:
  name: pacman-configmap-ttfdfdk5t8
---
apiVersion: apps/v1
kind: Deployment
metadata:
  labels:
    app.kubernetes.io/name: pacman-kikd
  name: pacman-kikd
...
```

❶ Inherits from base

❷ Overrides value

In addition to setting configuration properties as literals, Kustomize supports defining them as *.properties* files.

Create a *connection.properties* file with two properties inside:

```
db-url=prod:4321/db
db-username=ada
```

The *kustomization.yaml* file uses the files field instead of literals:

```
apiVersion: kustomize.config.k8s.io/v1beta1
kind: Kustomization
resources:
- ./deployment.yaml
configMapGenerator:
- name: pacman-configmap
  files: ❶
  - ./connection.properties ❷
```

❶   Sets a list of files to read

❷   Path to the properties file

Running the `kustomize build` command produces a `ConfigMap` containing the name of the file as a key, and the value as the content of the file:

```
apiVersion: v1
data:
  connection.properties: |-
    db-url=prod:4321/db
    db-username=ada
kind: ConfigMap
metadata:
  name: pacman-configmap-g9dm2gtt77
---
apiVersion: apps/v1
kind: Deployment
metadata:
  labels:
    app.kubernetes.io/name: pacman-kikd
  name: pacman-kikd
...
```

See Also

Kustomize offers a similar way to deal with Kubernetes Secrets. But as we'll see in Chapter 8, the best way to deal with Kubernetes Secrets is using Sealed Secrets.

4.6 Final Thoughts

Kustomize is a simple tool, using template-less technology that allows you to define plain YAML files and override values either using a merge strategy or using JSON Patch expressions. The structure of a project is free as you define the directory layout you feel most comfortable with; the only requirement is the presence of a *kustomization.yaml* file.

But there is another well-known tool to manage Kubernetes resources files, that in our opinion, is a bit more complicated but more powerful, especially when the application/service to deploy has several dependencies such as databases, mail servers, caches, etc. This tool is Helm, and we'll cover it in Chapter 5.

## CHAPTER 5

Helm

In Chapter 4, you learned about Kustomize, a simple yet powerful tool to manage Kubernetes resources. But another popular tool aims to simplify the Kubernetes resources management too: Helm.

Helm works similarly to Kustomize, but it's a template solution and acts more like a package manager, producing artifacts that are versionable, sharable, or deployable.

In this chapter, we'll introduce Helm, a package manager for Kubernetes that helps install and manage Kubernetes applications using the Go template language in YAML files.

The first step is to create a Helm project and deploy it to a Kubernetes cluster (see Recipes 5.1 and 5.2). After the first deployment, the application is updated with a new container image, a new configuration value, or any other field, such as the replica number (see Recipe 5.3).

One of the differences between Kustomize and Helm is the concept of a Chart. A Chart is a packaged artifact that can be shared and contains multiple elements like dependencies on other Charts (see Recipes 5.4, 5.5, and 5.6).

Application configuration values are properties usually mapped as a Kubernetes ConfigMap. Any change (and its consequent update on the cluster) on a ConfigMap doesn't trigger a rolling update of the application, which means that the application will run with the previous version until you manually restart it.

Helm provides some functions to automatically execute a rolling update when the ConfigMap of an application changes (see Recipe 5.7).

5.1 Creating a Helm Project

Problem

You want to create a simple Helm project.

Solution

Use the Helm (*https://helm.sh*) CLI tool to create a new project.

In contrast to Kustomize, which can be used either within the `kubectl` command or as a standalone CLI tool, Helm needs to be downloaded and installed in your local machine.

Helm is a packager for Kubernetes that bundles related manifest files and packages them into a single logical deployment unit: a Chart. Thus simplified, for many engineers, Helm makes it easy to start using Kubernetes with real applications.

Helm Charts are useful for addressing the installation complexities and simple upgrades of applications.

For this book, we use Helm 3.7.2, which you can download from GitHub (*https://oreil.ly/AWfiO*) and install in your PATH directory.

Open a terminal and run the following commands to create a Helm Chart directory layout:

```
mkdir pacman
mkdir pacman/templates

cd pacman
```

Then create three files: one that defines the Chart, another representing the deployment template using the Go template language and template functions from the Sprig library, and finally a file containing the default values for the Chart.

A *Chart.yaml* file declares the Chart with information such as version or name. Create the file in the root directory:

```
apiVersion: v2
name: pacman
description: A Helm chart for Pacman

type: application

version: 0.1.0  ❶

appVersion: "1.0.0"  ❷
```

❶ Version of the Chart. This is updated when something in the Chart definition is changed.

❷ Version of the application.

Let's create a *deployment.yaml* and a *service.yaml* template file to deploy the application.

The *deployment.yaml* file templatizes the deployment's name, the application version, the replica count, the container image and tag, the pull policy, the security context, and the port:

```
apiVersion: apps/v1
kind: Deployment
metadata:
  name: {{ .Chart.Name}} ❶
  labels:
    app.kubernetes.io/name: {{ .Chart.Name}}
    {{- if .Chart.AppVersion }} ❷
    app.kubernetes.io/version: {{ .Chart.AppVersion | quote }} ❸
    {{- end }}
spec:
  replicas: {{ .Values.replicaCount }} ❹
  selector:
    matchLabels:
      app.kubernetes.io/name: {{ .Chart.Name}}
  template:
    metadata:
      labels:
        app.kubernetes.io/name: {{ .Chart.Name}}
    spec:
      containers:
        - image: "{{ .Values.image.repository }}:
          {{ .Values.image.tag | default .Chart.AppVersion}}" ❺ ❻
          imagePullPolicy: {{ .Values.image.pullPolicy }} ❼
          securityContext:
            {{- toYaml .Values.securityContext | nindent 14 }}
          name: {{ .Chart.Name}}
          ports:
            - containerPort: {{ .Values.image.containerPort }}
              name: http
              protocol: TCP
```

❶ Sets the name from the *Chart.yaml* file

❷ Conditionally sets the version based on the presence of the appVersion in the *Chart.yaml* file

❸ Sets the appVersion value but quoting the property

❹   Placeholder for the `replicaCount` property

❺   Placeholder for the container image

❻   Placeholder for the image tag if present and if not, defaults to the *Chart.yaml* property

❼   Sets the `securityContext` value as a YAML object and not as a string, indenting it 14 spaces

The *service.yaml* file templatizes the service name and the container port:

```
apiVersion: v1
kind: Service
metadata:
  labels:
    app.kubernetes.io/name: {{ .Chart.Name }}
  name: {{ .Chart.Name }}
spec:
  ports:
    - name: http
      port: {{ .Values.image.containerPort }}
      targetPort: {{ .Values.image.containerPort }}
  selector:
    app.kubernetes.io/name: {{ .Chart.Name }}
```

The *values.yaml* file contains the default values for the Chart. These values can be overridden at runtime, but they provide good initial values.

Create the file in the root directory with some default values:

```
image: ❶
  repository: quay.io/gitops-cookbook/pacman-kikd ❷
  tag: "1.0.0"
  pullPolicy: Always
  containerPort: 8080

replicaCount: 1
securityContext: {} ❸
```

❶   Defines the `image` section

❷   Sets the `repository` property

❸   Empty `securityContext`

Built-in properties are capitalized; for this reason, properties defined in the *Chart.yaml* file start with an uppercase letter.

Since the `toYaml` function is used for the `securityContext` value, the expected value for the `securityContext` property in *values.yaml* should be a YAML object. For example:

```
securityContext:
  capabilities:
    drop:
    - ALL
  readOnlyRootFilesystem: true
  runAsNonRoot: true
  runAsUser: 1000
```

The relationship between all elements is shown in Figure 5-1.

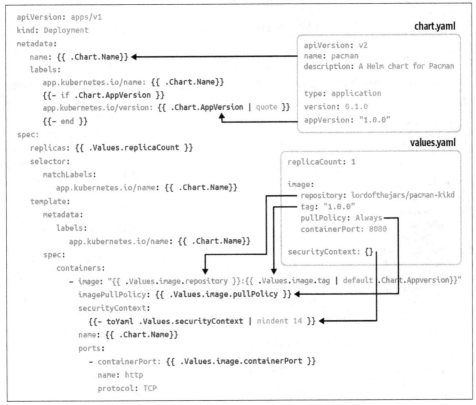

Figure 5-1. Relationship between Helm elements

At this point the Helm directory layout is created and should be similar to this:

```
pacman
    ├── Chart.yaml ❶
    ├── templates ❷
    │    ├── deployment.yaml ❸
    │    ├── service.yaml
    └── values.yaml ❹
```

❶ The *Chart.yaml* file is the Chart descriptor and contains metadata related to the Chart.

❷ The *templates* directory contains all template files used for installing a Chart.

❸ These files are Helm template files used to deploy the application.

❹ The *values.yaml* file contains the default values for a Chart.

To render the Helm Chart locally to YAML, run the following command in a terminal window:

```
helm template .
```

The output is:

```
---
apiVersion: v1
kind: Service
metadata:
  labels:
    app.kubernetes.io/name: pacman
  name: pacman ❶
spec:
  ports:
    - name: http
      port: 8080 ❷
      targetPort: 8080
  selector:
    app.kubernetes.io/name: pacman
---
apiVersion: apps/v1
kind: Deployment
metadata:
  name: pacman
  labels:
    app.kubernetes.io/name: pacman
    app.kubernetes.io/version: "1.0.0" ❸
spec:
  replicas: 1
  selector:
    matchLabels:
      app.kubernetes.io/name: pacman
  template:
```

```
metadata:
  labels:
    app.kubernetes.io/name: pacman
spec:
  containers:
    - image: "quay.io/gitops-cookbook/pacman-kikd:1.0.0" ❹
      imagePullPolicy: Always
      securityContext: ❺
        {}
      name: pacman
      ports:
        - containerPort: 8080
          name: http
          protocol: TCP
```

❶ Name is injected from *Chart.yaml*

❷ Port is set in *values.yaml*

❸ Version is taken from Chart version

❹ Concatenates content from two attributes

❺ Empty security context

You can override any default value by using the `--set` parameter in Helm. Let's override the `replicaCount` value from one (defined in *values.yaml*) to three:

```
helm template --set replicaCount=3 .
```

And the `replicas` value is updated:

```
apiVersion: apps/v1
kind: Deployment
metadata:
  name: pacman
  labels:
    app.kubernetes.io/name: pacman
    app.kubernetes.io/version: "1.0.0"
spec:
  replicas: 3
...
```

Discussion

Helm is a package manager for Kubernetes, and as such, it helps you with the task of versioning, sharing, and upgrading Kubernetes applications.

Let's see how to install the Helm Chart to a Kubernetes cluster and upgrade the application.

With Minikube up and running, execute the following command in a terminal window, and run the `install` command to deploy the application to the cluster:

```
helm install pacman .
```

The Chart is installed in the running Kubernetes instance:

```
LAST DEPLOYED: Sat Jan 22 15:13:50 2022
NAMESPACE: default
STATUS: deployed
REVISION: 1
TEST SUITE: None
```

Get the list of current deployed pods, Deployments, and Services to validate that the Helm Chart is deployed in the Kubernetes cluster:

```
kubectl get pods

NAME                      READY   STATUS    RESTARTS   AGE
pacman-7947b988-kzjbc     1/1     Running   0          60s

kubectl get deployment

NAME     READY   UP-TO-DATE   AVAILABLE   AGE
pacman   1/1     1            1           4m50s

kubectl get services

NAME     TYPE        CLUSTER-IP       EXTERNAL-IP   PORT(S)    AGE
pacman   ClusterIP   172.30.129.123   <none>        8080/TCP   9m55s
```

Also, it's possible to get history information about the deployed Helm Chart using the `history` command:

```
helm history pacman

REVISION        UPDATED                           STATUS        CHART          ↳
    APP VERSION DESCRIPTION
1                       Sat Jan 22 15:23:22 2022  deployed      pacman-0.1.0↳
    1.0.0               Install complete
```

To uninstall a Chart from the cluster, run `uninstall` command:

```
helm uninstall pacman

release "pacman" uninstalled
```

Helm is a package manager that lets you share the Chart (package) to other Charts as a dependency. For example, you can have a Chart defining the deployment of the application and another Chart as a dependency setting a database deployment. In this way, the installation process installs the application and the database Chart automatically.

We'll learn about the packaging process and adding dependencies in a later section.

You can use the `helm create <name>` command to let the Helm tool skaffold the project.

See Also

- Helm (*https://helm.sh*)
- Go template package (*https://oreil.ly/vYI40*)
- Sprig Function Documentation (*https://oreil.ly/ngC2v*)

5.2 Reusing Statements Between Templates

Problem

You want to reuse template statements across several files.

Solution

Use *_helpers.tpl* to define reusable statements.

We deployed a simple application to Kubernetes using Helm in the previous recipe. This simple application was composed of a Kubernetes Deployment file and a Kubernetes Service file where the `selector` field was defined with the same value.

As a reminder:

```
...
spec:
  replicas: {{ .Values.replicaCount }}
  selector:
    matchLabels:
      app.kubernetes.io/name: {{ .Chart.Name}}
  template:
    metadata:
      labels:
        app.kubernetes.io/name: {{ .Chart.Name}}
...

service.yaml
---
...
selector:
    app.kubernetes.io/name: {{ .Chart.Name }}
---
```

If you need to update this field—for example, adding a new label as a selector—you would need to update in three places, as shown in the previous snippets.

Helm lets you create a _helpers.tpl file in the *templates* directory defining statements that can be called in templates to avoid this problem.

Let's refactor the previous example to use the _helpers.tpl file to define the selector Labels.

Create the _helpers.tpl file in the *templates* directory with the following content:

```
{{- define "pacman.selectorLabels" -}} ❶
app.kubernetes.io/name: {{ .Chart.Name}} ❷
{{- end }}
```

❶ Defines the statement name

❷ Defines the logic of the statement

Then replace the template placeholders shown in previous snippets with a call to the podman.selectorLabels helper statement using the include keyword:

```
spec:
  replicas: {{ .Values.replicaCount }}
  selector:
    matchLabels:
      {{- include "pacman.selectorLabels" . | nindent 6 }} ❶
  template:
    metadata:
      labels:
        {{- include "pacman.selectorLabels" . | nindent 8 }} ❷
    spec:
      containers:
```

❶ Calls pacman.selectorLabels with indentation

❷ Calls pacman.selectorLabels with indentation

To render the Helm Chart locally to YAML, run the following command in a terminal window:

```
helm template .
```

The output is:

```
apiVersion: v1
kind: Service
metadata:
  labels:
    app.kubernetes.io/name: pacman
  name: pacman
spec:
  ports:
    - name: http
      port: 8080
      targetPort: 8080
```

```
    selector:
      app.kubernetes.io/name: pacman ❶
---
apiVersion: apps/v1
kind: Deployment
metadata:
  name: pacman
  labels:
    app.kubernetes.io/name: pacman
    app.kubernetes.io/version: "1.0.0"
spec:
  replicas: 1
  selector:
    matchLabels:
      app.kubernetes.io/name: pacman ❷
  template:
    metadata:
      labels:
        app.kubernetes.io/name: pacman ❸
    spec:
      containers:
        - image: "quay.io/gitops-cookbook/pacman-kikd:1.0.0"
          imagePullPolicy: Always
          securityContext:
            {}
          name: pacman
          ports:
            - containerPort: 8080
              name: http
              protocol: TCP
```

❶ Selector is updated with value set in _helpers.tpl

❷ Selector is updated with value set in _helpers.tpl

❸ Selector is updated with value set in _helpers.tpl

Discussion

If you want to update the selector labels, the only change you need to do is an update
to the _helpers.tpl file:

```
{{- define "pacman.selectorLabels" -}}
app.kubernetes.io/name: {{ .Chart.Name}}
app.kubernetes.io/version: {{ .Chart.AppVersion}} ❶
{{- end }}
```

❶ Adds a new attribute

To render the Helm Chart locally to YAML, run the following command in a terminal window:

```
helm template .
```

The output is:

```
---
# Source: pacman/templates/service.yaml
apiVersion: v1
kind: Service
metadata:
...
  selector:
    app.kubernetes.io/name: pacman
    app.kubernetes.io/version: 1.0.0  ❶
---
apiVersion: apps/v1
kind: Deployment
metadata:
  name: pacman
  labels:
    app.kubernetes.io/name: pacman
    app.kubernetes.io/version: "1.0.0"
spec:
  replicas: 1
  selector:
    matchLabels:
      app.kubernetes.io/name: pacman
      app.kubernetes.io/version: 1.0.0  ❷
  template:
    metadata:
      labels:
        app.kubernetes.io/name: pacman
        app.kubernetes.io/version: 1.0.0  ❸
    spec:
...
```

❶ Label is added

❷ Label is added

❸ Label is added

Although it's common to use __helpers.tpl_ as the filename to define functions, you can name any file starting with __, and Helm will read the functions too.

5.3 Updating a Container Image in Helm

Problem

You want to update the container image from a deployment file using Helm and upgrade the running instance.

Solution

Use the `upgrade` command.

With Minikube up and running, deploy version 1.0.0 of the `pacman` application:

```
helm install pacman .
```

With the first revision deployed, let's update the container image to a new version and deploy it.

You can check revision number by running the following command:

```
helm history pacman
```

```
REVISION   UPDATED                  STATUS     CHART          APP VERSION↳
   DESCRIPTION
1          Sun Jan 23 16:00:09 2022 deployed   pacman-0.1.0   1.0.0↳
   Install complete
```

To update the version, open *values.yaml* and update the `image.tag` field to the newer container image tag:

```
image:
  repository: quay.io/gitops-cookbook/pacman-kikd
  tag: "1.1.0" ❶
  pullPolicy: Always
  containerPort: 8080

replicaCount: 1
securityContext: {}
```

❶   Updates to container tag to 1.1.0

Then update the `appVersion` field of the *Chart.yaml* file:

```
apiVersion: v2
name: pacman
description: A Helm chart for Pacman

type: application
version: 0.1.0
appVersion: "1.1.0" ❶
```

❶   Version is updated accordingly

You can use `appVersion` as the tag instead of having two separate fields. Using two fields or one might depend on your use case, versioning strategy, and lifecycle of your software.

After these changes, upgrade the deployment by running the following command:

```
helm upgrade pacman .
```

The output reflects that a new revision has been deployed:

```
Release "pacman" has been upgraded. Happy Helming!
NAME: pacman
LAST DEPLOYED: Mon Jan 24 11:39:28 2022
NAMESPACE: asotobue-dev
STATUS: deployed
REVISION: 2 ❶
TEST SUITE: None
```

❶ New revision

The `history` command shows all changes between all versions:

```
helm history pacman

REVISION UPDATED                        STATUS      CHART          APP VERSION↵
DESCRIPTION
1        Mon Jan 24 10:22:06 2022 superseded  pacman-0.1.0   1.0.0↵
Install complete
2        Mon Jan 24 11:39:28 2022 deployed    pacman-0.1.0   1.1.0↵
Upgrade complete
```

 `appVersion` is the application version, so every time you change the application version, you should update that field too. On the other side, `version` is the Chart version and should be updated when the definition of the Chart (i.e., templates) changes, so both fields are independent.

Discussion

Not only you can install or upgrade a version with Helm, but you can also roll back to a previous revision.

In the terminal window, run the following command:

```
helm rollback pacman 1
```

```
Rollback was a success! Happy Helming!
```

Running the `history` command reflects this change too:

```
helm history pacman

REVISION  UPDATED                     STATUS      CHART         APP VERSION↵
DESCRIPTION
1         Mon Jan 24 10:22:06 2022    superseded  pacman-0.1.0  1.0.0↵
Install complete
2         Mon Jan 24 11:39:28 2022    superseded  pacman-0.1.0  1.1.0↵
Upgrade complete
3         Mon Jan 24 12:31:58 2022    deployed    pacman-0.1.0  1.0.0↵
Rollback to
```

Finally, Helm offers a way to override values, not only using the `--set` argument as shown in Recipe 5.1, but by providing a YAML file.

Create a new YAML file named *newvalues.yaml* in the root directory with the following content:

```
image:
  tag: "1.2.0"
```

Then run the `template` command, setting the new file as an override of *values.yaml*:

```
helm template pacman -f newvalues.yaml .
```

The resulting YAML document is using the values set in *values.yaml* but overriding the `images.tag` set in *newvalues.yaml*:

```
apiVersion: apps/v1
kind: Deployment
metadata:
  name: pacman
...
spec:
  replicas: 1
  selector:
    matchLabels:
      app.kubernetes.io/name: pacman
  template:
    metadata:
      labels:
        app.kubernetes.io/name: pacman
    spec:
      containers:
        - image: "quay.io/gitops-cookbook/pacman-kikd:1.2.0"
          imagePullPolicy: Always
...
```

5.4 Packaging and Distributing a Helm Chart

Problem

You want to package and distribute a Helm Chart so it can be reused by others.

Solution

Use the `package` command.

Helm is a package manager for Kubernetes. As we've seen in this chapter, the basic unit in Helm is a Chart containing the Kubernetes files required to deploy the application, the default values for the templates, etc.

But we've not yet seen how to package Helm Charts and distribute them to be available to other Charts as dependencies or deployed by other users.

Let's package the `pacman` Chart into a *.tgz* file. In the *pacman* directory, run the following command:

```
helm package .
```

And you'll get a message informing you where the archive is stored:

```
Successfully packaged chart and saved it to:↵
gitops-cookbook/code/05_helm/04_package/pacman/pacman-0.1.0.tgz
```

A Chart then needs to be published into a Chart repository. A Chart repository is an HTTP server with an *index.yaml* file containing metadata information regarding Charts and *.tgz* Charts.

To publish them, update the *index.yaml* file with the new metadata information, and upload the artifact.

The directory layout of a repository might look like this:

```
repo
├── index.yaml
├── pacman-0.1.0.tgz
```

The *index.yaml* file with information about each Chart present in the repository looks like:

```
apiVersion: v1
entries:
  pacman:
  - apiVersion: v2
    appVersion: 1.0.0
    created: "2022-01-24T16:42:54.080959+01:00"
    description: A Helm chart for Pacman
    digest: aa3cce809ffcca86172fc793d7804d1c61f157b9b247680a67d5b16b18a0798d
    name: pacman
```

```
    type: application
    urls:
    - pacman-0.1.0.tgz
    version: 0.1.0
generated: "2022-01-24T16:42:54.080485+01:00"
```

 You can run `helm repo index` in the root directory, where packaged Charts are stored, to generate the index file automatically.

Discussion

In addition to packaging a Helm Chart, Helm can generate a signature file for the
packaged Chart to verify its correctness later.

In this way, you can be sure it has not been modified, and it's the correct Chart.

To sign/verify the package, you need a pair of GPG keys in the machine; we're
assuming you already have one pair created.

Now you need to call the `package` command but set the `-sign` argument with the
required parameters to generate a signature file:

```
helm package --sign --key 'me@example.com' \
    --keyring /home/me/.gnupg/secring.gpg  .
```

Now, two files are created—the packaged Helm Chart (*.tgz*) and the signature file
(*.tgz.prov*):

```
.
├── Chart.yaml
├── pacman-0.1.0.tgz ❶
├── pacman-0.1.0.tgz.prov ❷
├── templates
│   ├── deployment.yaml
│   └── service.yaml
└── values.yaml
```

❶ Chart package

❷ Signature file

 Remember to upload both files in the Chart repository.

To verify that a Chart is valid and has not been manipulated, use the `verify` command:

```
helm verify pacman-0.1.0.tgz

Signed by: alexs (book) <asotobu@example.com>
Using Key With Fingerprint: 57C4511D738BC0B288FAF9D69B40EB787040F3CF
Chart Hash Verified:↳
     sha256:d8b2e0c5e12a8425df2ea3a903807b93aabe4a6ff8277511a7865c847de3c0bf  ❶
```

❶ It's valid

See Also

- The Chart Repository Guide (*https://oreil.ly/pQ2Ab*)
- Helm Provenance and Integrity (*https://oreil.ly/1Hql0*)

5.5 Deploying a Chart from a Repository

Problem

You want to deploy a Helm Chart stored in Chart repository.

Solution

Use the `repo add` command to add the remote repository and the `install` command to deploy it.

Public Helm Chart repositories like Bitnami (*https://oreil.ly/QJzWZ*) are available for this purpose.

To install Charts from a repository (either public or private), you need to register it using its URL:

```
helm repo add bitnami https://charts.bitnami.com/bitnami  ❶
```

❶ URL of Helm Chart repository where *index.yaml* is placed

List the registered repositories:

```
helm repo list

NAME          URL
stable        https://charts.helm.sh/stable
bitnami       https://charts.bitnami.com/bitnami  ❶
```

❶ Bitnami repo is registered

Run `helm repo update` to get the latest list of Charts for each repo.

After registering a repository, you might want to find which Charts are available.

If you want to deploy a PostgreSQL instance in the cluster, use the `search` command to search all repositories for a Chart that matches the name:

```
helm search repo postgresql
```

The outputs are the list of Charts that matches the name, the version of the Chart and PostgreSQL, and a description. Notice the name of the Chart is composed of the repository name and the Chart name, i.e., `bitnami/postgresql`:

```
NAME                                CHART VERSION   APP VERSION↳
        DESCRIPTION
bitnami/postgresql                  10.16.2         11.14.0↳
        Chart for PostgreSQL, an object-relational data...
bitnami/postgresql-ha               8.2.6           11.14.0↳
        Chart for PostgreSQL with HA architecture (usin...
stable/postgresql                   8.6.4           11.7.0↳
        DEPRECATED Chart for PostgreSQL, an object-rela...
stable/pgadmin                      1.2.2           4.18.0↳
        pgAdmin is a web based administration tool for ...
stable/stolon                       1.6.5           0.16.0↳
        DEPRECATED - Stolon - PostgreSQL cloud native H...
stable/gcloud-sqlproxy              0.6.1           1.11↳
        DEPRECATED Google Cloud SQL Proxy
stable/prometheus-postgres-exporter 1.3.1           0.8.0↳
        DEPRECATED A Helm chart for prometheus postgres...
```

To deploy the PostgreSQL Chart, run the `install` command but change the location of the Helm Chart from a local directory to the full name of the Chart (`<repo>/<chart>`):

```
helm install my-db \ ❶
--set postgresql.postgresqlUsername=my-default,postgresql.↳
postgresqlPassword=postgres,postgresql.postgresqlDatabase=mydb,↳
postgresql.persistence.enabled=false \ ❷
bitnami/postgresql ❸
```

❶ Sets the name of the deployment

❷ Overrides default values to the ones set in the command line

❸ Sets the PostgreSQL Chart stored in the Bitnami repo

And a detailed output is shown in the console:

```
NAME: my-db
LAST DEPLOYED: Mon Jan 24 22:33:56 2022
NAMESPACE: asotobue-dev
STATUS: deployed
REVISION: 1
TEST SUITE: None
NOTES:
CHART NAME: postgresql
CHART VERSION: 10.16.2
APP VERSION: 11.14.0

** Please be patient while the chart is being deployed **

PostgreSQL can be accessed via port 5432 on the following DNS names↵
from within your cluster:

    my-db-postgresql.asotobue-dev.svc.cluster.local - Read/Write connection

To get the((("passwords", "Helm Charts")))((("Helm", "Charts", "pass-
words")))((("Charts", "passwords"))) password for "postgres" run:

    export POSTGRES_ADMIN_PASSWORD=$(kubectl get secret↵
     --namespace asotobue-dev my-db-postgresql -o↵
     jsonpath="{.data.postgresql-postgres-password}" | base64 --decode)

To get the password for "my-default" run:

    export POSTGRES_PASSWORD=$(kubectl get secret↵
     --namespace asotobue-dev my-db-postgresql -o↵
     jsonpath="{.data.postgresql-password}" | base64 --decode)

To connect to your database run the following command:

    kubectl run my-db-postgresql-client --rm --tty -i --restart='Never'↵
     --namespace asotobue-dev↵
     --image docker.io/bitnami/postgresql:11.14.0-debian-10-r28↵
     --env="PGPASSWORD=$POSTGRES_PASSWORD"↵
     --command -- psql --host my-db-postgresql -U my-default -d mydb↵
     -p 5432


To connect to your ((("Helm", "Charts", "connecting to databases")))((("Charts",
"databases", "connecting to")))((("databases", "connecting to", "Helm
Charts")))database from outside the cluster execute the following commands:

    kubectl port-forward --namespace asotobue-dev svc/my-db-postgresql 5432:5432 &
    PGPASSWORD="$POSTGRES_PASSWORD" psql --host 127.0.0.1 -U my-default -d mydb -p
5432
```

Inspect the installation by listing pods, Services, StatefulSets, or Secrets:

```
kubectl get pods

NAME                    READY   STATUS    RESTARTS   AGE
my-db-postgresql-0      1/1     Running   0          23s

kubectl get services

NAME                         TYPE        CLUSTER-IP     EXTERNAL-IP   PORT(S)     AGE
my-db-postgresql             ClusterIP   172.30.35.1    <none>        5432/TCP
3m33s
my-db-postgresql-headless    ClusterIP   None           <none>        5432/TCP
3m33s

kubectl get statefulset

NAME                READY   AGE
my-db-postgresql    1/1     4m24s

kubectl get secrets

NAME                            TYPE                DATA   AGE
my-db-postgresql                Opaque              2      5m23s
sh.helm.release.v1.my-db.v1     helm.sh/release.v1  1      5m24s
```

Discussion

When a third party creates a Chart, there is no direct access to default values or the
list of parameters to override. Helm provides a show command to check these values:

```
helm show values bitnami/postgresql
```

And shows all the possible values:

```
## @section Global parameters
## Global Docker image parameters
## Please, note that this will override the image parameters, including dependen
cies
## configured to use the global value
## Current available global Docker image parameters: imageRegistry, imagePullSe
crets
## and storageClass
##

## @param global.imageRegistry Global Docker image registry
## @param global.imagePullSecrets Global Docker registry secret names as an array
## @param global.storageClass Global StorageClass for Persistent Volume(s)
##
global:
  imageRegistry: ""
  ## E.g.
  ## imagePullSecrets:
  ##    - myRegistryKeySecretName
  ##
  imagePullSecrets: []
...
```

5.6 Deploying a Chart with a Dependency

Problem

You want to deploy a Helm Chart that is a dependency of another Chart.

Solution

Use the dependencies section in the *Chart.yaml* file to register other Charts. So far, we've seen how to deploy simple services to the cluster, but usually a service might have other dependencies like a database, mail server, distributed cache, etc.

In the previous section, we saw how to deploy a PostgreSQL server in a Kubernetes cluster. In this section, we'll see how to deploy a service composed of a Java service returning a list of songs stored in a PostgreSQL database. The application is summarized in Figure 5-2.

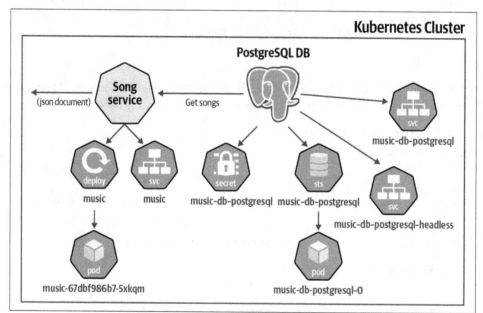

Figure 5-2. Music application overview

Let's start creating the Chart layout shown in Recipe 5.1:

```
mkdir music
mkdir music/templates

cd music
```

Then create two template files to deploy the music service.

The *templates/deployment.yaml* file contains the Kubernetes Deployment definition:

```
apiVersion: apps/v1
kind: Deployment
metadata:
  name: {{ .Chart.Name}}
  labels:
    app.kubernetes.io/name: {{ .Chart.Name}}
    {{- if .Chart.AppVersion }}
    app.kubernetes.io/version: {{ .Chart.AppVersion | quote }}
    {{- end }}
spec:
  replicas: {{ .Values.replicaCount }}
  selector:
    matchLabels:
      app.kubernetes.io/name: {{ .Chart.Name}}
  template:
    metadata:
      labels:
        app.kubernetes.io/name: {{ .Chart.Name}}
    spec:
      containers:
        - image: "{{ .Values.image.repository }}:↳
          {{ .Values.image.tag | default .Chart.AppVersion}}"
          imagePullPolicy: {{ .Values.image.pullPolicy }}
          name: {{ .Chart.Name}}
          ports:
            - containerPort: {{ .Values.image.containerPort }}
              name: http
              protocol: TCP
          env:
            - name: QUARKUS_DATASOURCE_JDBC_URL
              value: {{ .Values.postgresql.server | ↳
              default (printf "%s-postgresql" ( .Release.Name )) | quote }}
            - name: QUARKUS_DATASOURCE_USERNAME
              value: {{ .Values.postgresql.postgresqlUsername | ↳
              default (printf "postgres" ) | quote }}
            - name: QUARKUS_DATASOURCE_PASSWORD
              valueFrom:
                secretKeyRef:
                  name: {{ .Values.postgresql.secretName | ↳
                  default (printf "%s-postgresql" ( .Release.Name )) | quote }}
                  key: {{ .Values.postgresql.secretKey }}
```

The *templates/service.yaml* file contains the Kubernetes Service definition:

```
apiVersion: v1
kind: Service
metadata:
  labels:
    app.kubernetes.io/name: {{ .Chart.Name }}
  name: {{ .Chart.Name }}
spec:
  ports:
    - name: http
```

```
      port: {{ .Values.image.containerPort }}
      targetPort: {{ .Values.image.containerPort }}
    selector:
      app.kubernetes.io/name: {{ .Chart.Name }}
```

After the creation of the templates, it's time for the Chart metadata *Chart.yaml* file. In this case, we need to define the dependencies of this Chart too. Since the music service uses a PostgreSQL database, we can add the Chart used in Recipe 5.5 as a dependency:

```
apiVersion: v2
name: music
description: A Helm chart for Music service

type: application
version: 0.1.0
appVersion: "1.0.0"

dependencies: ❶
  - name: postgresql ❷
    version: 10.16.2 ❸
    repository: "https://charts.bitnami.com/bitnami" ❹
```

❶ Dependencies section

❷ Name of the Chart to add as dependency

❸ Chart version

❹ Repository

The final file is *Values.yaml* with default configuration values. In this case, a new section is added to configure music deployment with PostgreSQL instance parameters:

```
image:
  repository: quay.io/gitops-cookbook/music
  tag: "1.0.0"
  pullPolicy: Always
  containerPort: 8080

replicaCount: 1

postgresql: ❶
  server: jdbc:postgresql://music-db-postgresql:5432/mydb
  postgresqlUsername: my-default
  secretName: music-db-postgresql
  secretKey: postgresql-password
```

❶ PostgreSQL section

With the Chart in place, the next thing to do is download the dependency Chart and store it in the *charts* directory. This process is automatically done by running the dependency update command:

```
helm dependency update
```

The command output shows that one Chart has been downloaded and saved:

```
Hang tight while we grab the latest from your chart repositories...
...Successfully got an update from the "stable" chart repository
...Successfully got an update from the "bitnami" chart repository
Update Complete. ❋Happy Helming!❋
Saving 1 charts
Downloading postgresql from repo https://charts.bitnami.com/bitnami
Deleting outdated charts
```

The directory layout looks like this:

```
music
├── Chart.lock
├── Chart.yaml
├── charts
│   └── postgresql-10.16.2.tgz ❶
├── templates
│   ├── deployment.yaml
│   └── service.yaml
└── values.yaml
```

❶ PostgreSQL Chart is placed in the correct directory

Finally, we deploy the Chart, setting configuration PostgreSQL deployment values from the command line:

```
helm install music-db --set postgresql.postgresqlPassword=postgres postgresql.post-
gresqlDatabase=mydb,postgresql.persistence.enabled=false .
```

The installation process shows information about the deployment:

```
NAME: music-db
LAST DEPLOYED: Tue Jan 25 17:53:17 2022
NAMESPACE: default
STATUS: deployed
REVISION: 1
TEST SUITE: None
```

Inspect the installation by listing pods, Services, StatefulSets, or Secrets:

```
kubectl get pods

NAME                       READY   STATUS    RESTARTS      AGE
music-67dbf986b7-5xkqm     1/1     Running   1 (32s ago)   39s
music-db-postgresql-0      1/1     Running   0             39s

kubectl get statefulset
```

```
NAME                  READY   AGE
music-db-postgresql   1/1     53s

kubectl get services

NAME                             TYPE        CLUSTER-IP     EXTERNAL-IP   PORT(S)    AGE
kubernetes                       ClusterIP   10.96.0.1      <none>        443/TCP    40d
music                            ClusterIP   10.104.110.34  <none>        8080/TCP   82s
music-db-postgresql              ClusterIP   10.110.71.13   <none>        5432/TCP   82s
music-db-postgresql-headless     ClusterIP   None           <none>        5432/TCP   82s
```

We can validate the access to the music service by using port forwarding to the Kubernetes Service.

Open a new terminal window and run the following command:

```
kubectl port-forward service/music 8080:8080

Forwarding from 127.0.0.1:8080 -> 8080
Forwarding from [::1]:8080 -> 8080
```

The terminal is blocked and it's normal until you stop the kubectl port-forward process. Thanks to port forwarding, we can access the music service using the local host address and port 8080.

In another terminal, curl the service:

```
curl localhost:8080/song
```

The request is sent to the music service deployed in Kubernetes and returns a list of songs:

```
[
  {
    "id": 1,
    "artist": "DT",
    "name": "Quiero Munchies"
  },
  {
    "id": 2,
    "artist": "Lin-Manuel Miranda",
    "name": "We Don't Talk About Bruno"
  },
  {
    "id": 3,
    "artist": "Imagination",
    "name": "Just An Illusion"
  },
  {
    "id": 4,
    "artist": "Txarango",
    "name": "Tanca Els Ulls"
  },
  {
    "id": 5,
```

```
    "artist": "Halsey",
    "name": "Could Have Been Me"
  }
]
```

5.7 Triggering a Rolling Update Automatically

Problem

You want to trigger a rolling update of deployment when a `ConfigMap` object is changed.

Solution

Use the `sha256sum` template function to generate a change on the deployment file.

In Recipe 4.5, we saw that Kustomize has a `ConfigMapGenerator` that automatically appends a hash to the `ConfigMap` metadata name and modifies the deployment file with the new hash when used. Any change on the `ConfigMap` triggers a rolling update of the deployment.

Helm doesn't provide a direct way like Kustomize does to update a deployment file when the `ConfigMap` changes, but there is a template function to calculate a SHA-256 hash of any file and embed the result in the template.

Suppose we've got a Node.js application that returns a greeting message. An environment variable configures this greeting message, and in the Kubernetes Deployment, this variable is injected from a Kubernetes `ConfigMap`.

Figure 5-3 shows an overview of the application.

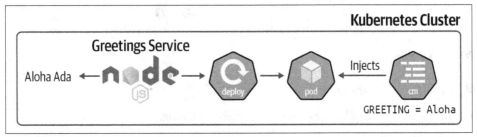

Figure 5-3. Greetings application overview

Let's create the Helm Chart for the Greetings application; note that we're not covering the entire process of creating a Chart, but just the essential parts. You can refer to Recipe 5.1 to get started.

Create a deployment template that injects a `ConfigMap` as an environment variable. The following listing shows the file:

```yaml
apiVersion: apps/v1
kind: Deployment
metadata:
  name: {{ .Chart.Name}}
  labels:
    app.kubernetes.io/name: {{ .Chart.Name}}
    {{- if .Chart.AppVersion }}
    app.kubernetes.io/version: {{ .Chart.AppVersion | quote }}
    {{- end }}
spec:
  replicas: {{ .Values.replicaCount }}
  selector:
    matchLabels:
      app.kubernetes.io/name: {{ .Chart.Name}}
  template:
    metadata:
      labels:
        app.kubernetes.io/name: {{ .Chart.Name}}
    spec:
      containers:
        - image: "{{ .Values.image.repository }}:↳
        {{ .Values.image.tag | default .Chart.AppVersion}}"
          imagePullPolicy: {{ .Values.image.pullPolicy }}
          name: {{ .Chart.Name}}
          ports:
            - containerPort: {{ .Values.image.containerPort }}
              name: http
              protocol: TCP
          env:
            - name: GREETING
              valueFrom:
                configMapKeyRef:
                  name: {{ .Values.configmap.name}} ❶
                  key: greeting ❷
```

❶ ConfigMap name

❷ Property key of the `ConfigMap`

The initial `ConfigMap` file is shown in the following listing:

```yaml
apiVersion: v1
kind: ConfigMap
metadata:
  name: greeting-config ❶
data:
  greeting: Aloha ❷
```

❶ Sets `ConfigMap` name

❷ Key/value

Create a Kubernetes Service template to access the service:

```
apiVersion: v1
kind: Service
metadata:
  labels:
    app.kubernetes.io/name: {{ .Chart.Name }}
  name: {{ .Chart.Name }}
spec:
  ports:
    - name: http
      port: {{ .Values.image.containerPort }}
      targetPort: {{ .Values.image.containerPort }}
  selector:
    app.kubernetes.io/name: {{ .Chart.Name }}
```

Update the *values.yaml* file with the template `configmap` parameters:

```
image:
  repository: quay.io/gitops-cookbook/greetings
  tag: "1.0.0"
  pullPolicy: Always
  containerPort: 8080

replicaCount: 1

configmap:
  name: greeting-config
```

❶ Refers to `ConfigMap` name

Finally, install the Chart using the `install` command:

```
helm install greetings .
```

When the Chart is deployed, use the `kubectl port-forward` command in one terminal to get access to the service:

```
kubectl port-forward service/greetings 8080:8080
```

And `curl` the service in another terminal window:

```
curl localhost:8080
Aloha Ada
```

❶ Configured greeting is used

Now, let's update the `ConfigMap` file to a new greeting message:

```
apiVersion: v1
kind: ConfigMap
metadata:
  name: greeting-config
data:
  greeting: Hola ❶
```

❶ New greeting message

Update the `appVersion` field from the *Chart.yaml* file to `1.0.1` and upgrade the Chart by running the following command:

```
helm upgrade greetings .
```

Restart the `kubectl port-forward` process and `curl` the service again:

```
curl localhost:8080
Aloha Alexandra ❶
```

❶ Greeting message isn't updated

The `ConfigMap` object is updated during the upgrade, but since there are no changes in the `Deployment` object, there is no restart of the pod; hence the environment variable is not set to the new value. Listing the pods shows no execution of the rolling update:

```
kubectl get pods
```

NAME	READY	STATUS	RESTARTS	AGE
greetings-64ddfcb649-m5pml	1/1	Running	0	2m21s ❶

❶ Age value shows no rolling update

Figure 5-4 summarizes the change.

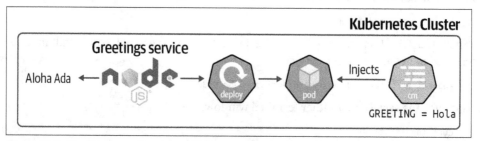

Figure 5-4. Greetings application with new configuration value

Let's use the `sha256sum` function to calculate an SHA-256 value of the *configmap.yaml* file content and set it as a pod annotation, which effectively triggers a rolling update as the pod definition has changed:

```
spec:
  replicas: {{ .Values.replicaCount }}
  selector:
    matchLabels:
      app.kubernetes.io/name: {{ .Chart.Name}}
  template:
    metadata:
      labels:
        app.kubernetes.io/name: {{ .Chart.Name}}
      annotations:
        checksum/config: {{ include (print $.Template.BasePath "/configmap.yaml")↳
          . | sha256sum }} ❶
```

❶ Includes the *configmap.yaml* file, calculates the SHA-256 value, and sets it as an annotation

Update the `ConfigMap` again with a new value:

```
apiVersion: v1
kind: ConfigMap
metadata:
  name: greeting-config
data:
  greeting: Namaste ❶
```

❶ New greeting message

Update the `appVersion` field from *Chart.yaml* to `1.0.1` and upgrade the Chart by running the following command:

```
helm upgrade greetings .
```

Restart the `kubectl port-forward` process and `curl` the service again:

```
curl localhost:8080
Namaste Alexandra ❶
```

❶ Greeting message is the new one

List the pods deployed in the cluster again, and you'll notice that a rolling update is happening:

```
kubectl get pods
```

NAME	READY	STATUS	RESTARTS	AGE
greetings-5c6b86dbbd-2p9bd	0/1	ContainerCreating	0	3s ❶
greetings-64ddfcb649-m5pml	1/1	Running	0	2m21s

❶ A rolling update is happening

Describe the pod to validate that the annotation with the SHA-256 value is present:

```
kubectl describe pod greetings-5c6b86dbbd-s4n7b
```

The output shows all pod parameters. The important one is the `annotations` placed at the top of the output showing the `checksum/config` annotation containing the calculated SHA-256 value:

```
Name:                  greetings-5c6b86dbbd-s4n7b
Namespace:             asotobue-dev
Priority:              -3
Priority Class Name:   sandbox-users-pods
Node:                  ip-10-0-186-34.ec2.internal/10.0.186.34
Start Time:            Thu, 27 Jan 2022 11:55:02 +0100
Labels:                app.kubernetes.io/name=greetings
                       pod-template-hash=5c6b86dbbd
Annotations:           checksum/config:↪
     59e9100616a11d65b691a914cd429dc6011a34e02465173f5f53584b4aa7cba8 ❶
```

❶ Calculated value

Figure 5-5 summarizes the elements that changed when the application was updated.

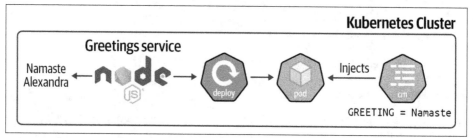

Figure 5-5. Final overview of the Greetings application

5.8 Final Thoughts

In the previous chapter, we saw Kustomize; in this chapter, we've seen another tool to help deploy Kubernetes applications.

When you need to choose between Kustomize or Helm, you might have questions on which one to use.

In our experience, the best way to proceed is with Kustomize for simple projects, where only simple changes might be required between new deployments.

If the project is complex with external dependencies, and several deployment parameters, then Helm is a better option.

## CHAPTER 6

Cloud Native CI/CD

In the previous chapter you learned about Helm, a popular templating system for Kubernetes. All the recipes from previous chapters represent a common tooling for creating and managing containers for Kubernetes, and now it's time to think about the automation on Kubernetes using such tools. Let's move our focus to the cloud native continuous integration/continuous deployment (CI/CD).

Continuous integration is an automated process that takes new code created by a developer and builds, tests, and runs that code. The cloud native CI refers to the model where cloud computing and cloud services are involved in this process. The benefits from this model are many, such as portable and reproducible workloads across clouds for highly scalable and on-demand use cases. And it also represents the building blocks for GitOps workflows as it enables automation through actions performed via Git.

Tekton (*https://tekton.dev*) is a popular open source implementation of a cloud native CI/CD system on top of Kubernetes. In fact, Tekton installs and runs as an extension on a Kubernetes cluster and comprises a set of Kubernetes Custom Resources that define the building blocks you can create and reuse for your pipelines.[1] (See Recipe 6.1.)

The Tekton engine lives inside a Kubernetes cluster and through its API objects represents a declarative way to define the actions to perform. The core components such as *Tasks* and *Pipelines* can be used to create a pipeline to generate artifacts and/or containers from a Git repository (see Recipes 6.2, 6.3, and 6.4).

Tekton also supports a mechanism for automating the start of a Pipeline with *Triggers*. These allow you to detect and extract information from events from a variety of

---

[1] See the Tekton documentation (*https://oreil.ly/NxpqN*).

sources, such as a webhook, and to start Tasks or Pipelines accordingly (see Recipe 6.8).

Working with private Git repositories is a common use case that Tekton supports nicely (see Recipe 6.4), and building artifacts and creating containers can be done in many ways such as with Buildah (see Recipe 6.5) or Shipwright, which we discussed in Chapter 3. It is also possible to integrate Kustomize (see Recipe 6.9) and Helm (see Recipe 6.10) in order to make the CI part dynamic and take benefit of the rich ecosystem of Kubernetes tools.

Tekton is Kubernetes-native solution, thus it's universal; however, it's not the only cloud native CI/CD citizen in the market. Other good examples for GitOps-ready workloads are Drone (Recipe 6.11) and GitHub Actions (Recipe 6.12).

6.1 Install Tekton

Problem

You want to install Tekton in order to have cloud native CI/CD on your Kubernetes cluster.

Solution

Tekton (*https://tekton.dev*) is a Kubernetes-native CI/CD solution that can be installed on top of any Kubernetes cluster. The installation brings you a set of Kubernetes Custom Resources (CRDs) (*https://oreil.ly/mv0cl*) that you can use to compose your Pipelines, as shown in Figure 6-1:

Task
> A reusable, loosely coupled number of steps that perform a specific function (e.g., building a container image). Tasks get executed as Kubernetes pods, while steps in a Task map onto containers.

Pipeline
> A list Tasks needed to build and/or deploy your apps.

TaskRun
> The execution and result of running an instance of a Task.

PipelineRun
> The execution and result of running an instance of a Pipeline, which includes a number of TaskRuns.

Trigger
> Detects an event and connects to other CRDs to specify what happens when such an event occurs.

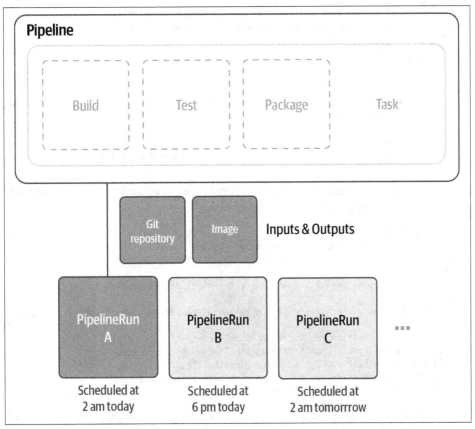

Figure 6-1. Tekton Pipelines

To install Tekton, you just need kubectl CLI and a Kubernetes cluster such as Minikube (see Chapter 2).

Tekton has a modular structure. You can install all components separately or all at once (e.g., with an Operator):

Tekton Pipelines
    Contains Tasks and Pipelines

Tekton Triggers
    Contains Triggers and EventListeners

Tekton Dashboard
    A convenient dashboard to visualize Pipelines and logs

Tekton CLI
    A CLI to manage Tekton objects (start/stop Pipelines and Tasks, check logs)

You can also use a Kubernetes Operator to install and manage Tekton components on your cluster. See more details on how from OperatorHub (*https://oreil.ly/6UoU3*).

First you need to install the Tekton Pipelines (*https://oreil.ly/oOL2V*) component. At the time of writing this book, we are using version 0.37.0:

```
kubectl apply \
-f https://storage.googleapis.com/tekton-releases/pipeline/previous/v0.37.0/
release.yaml
```

The installation will create a new Kubernetes namespace called `tekton-pipelines` and you should see output similar to the following:

```
namespace/tekton-pipelines created
podsecuritypolicy.policy/tekton-pipelines created
clusterrole.rbac.authorization.k8s.io/tekton-pipelines-controller-cluster-access
created
clusterrole.rbac.authorization.k8s.io/tekton-pipelines-controller-tenant-access
created
clusterrole.rbac.authorization.k8s.io/tekton-pipelines-webhook-cluster-access cre-
ated
role.rbac.authorization.k8s.io/tekton-pipelines-controller created
role.rbac.authorization.k8s.io/tekton-pipelines-webhook created
role.rbac.authorization.k8s.io/tekton-pipelines-leader-election created
role.rbac.authorization.k8s.io/tekton-pipelines-info created
serviceaccount/tekton-pipelines-controller created
serviceaccount/tekton-pipelines-webhook created
clusterrolebinding.rbac.authorization.k8s.io/tekton-pipelines-controller-cluster-
access created
clusterrolebinding.rbac.authorization.k8s.io/tekton-pipelines-controller-tenant-
access created
clusterrolebinding.rbac.authorization.k8s.io/tekton-pipelines-webhook-cluster-
access created
rolebinding.rbac.authorization.k8s.io/tekton-pipelines-controller created
rolebinding.rbac.authorization.k8s.io/tekton-pipelines-webhook created
rolebinding.rbac.authorization.k8s.io/tekton-pipelines-controller-leaderelection
created
rolebinding.rbac.authorization.k8s.io/tekton-pipelines-webhook-leaderelection cre-
ated
rolebinding.rbac.authorization.k8s.io/tekton-pipelines-info created
customresourcedefinition.apiextensions.k8s.io/clustertasks.tekton.dev created
customresourcedefinition.apiextensions.k8s.io/pipelines.tekton.dev created
customresourcedefinition.apiextensions.k8s.io/pipelineruns.tekton.dev created
customresourcedefinition.apiextensions.k8s.io/resolutionrequests.resolution.tek-
ton.dev created
customresourcedefinition.apiextensions.k8s.io/pipelineresources.tekton.dev created
customresourcedefinition.apiextensions.k8s.io/runs.tekton.dev created
customresourcedefinition.apiextensions.k8s.io/tasks.tekton.dev created
customresourcedefinition.apiextensions.k8s.io/taskruns.tekton.dev created
secret/webhook-certs created
```

```
validatingwebhookconfiguration.admissionregistration.k8s.io/validation.web-
hook.pipeline.tekton.dev created
mutatingwebhookconfiguration.admissionregistration.k8s.io/webhook.pipeline.tek-
ton.dev created
validatingwebhookconfiguration.admissionregistration.k8s.io/config.webhook.pipe-
line.tekton.dev created
clusterrole.rbac.authorization.k8s.io/tekton-aggregate-edit created
clusterrole.rbac.authorization.k8s.io/tekton-aggregate-view created
configmap/config-artifact-bucket created
configmap/config-artifact-pvc created
configmap/config-defaults created
configmap/feature-flags created
configmap/pipelines-info created
configmap/config-leader-election created
configmap/config-logging created
configmap/config-observability created
configmap/config-registry-cert created
deployment.apps/tekton-pipelines-controller created
service/tekton-pipelines-controller created
horizontalpodautoscaler.autoscaling/tekton-pipelines-webhook created
deployment.apps/tekton-pipelines-webhook created
service/tekton-pipelines-webhook created
```

You can monitor and verify the installation with the following command:

```
kubectl get pods -w -n tekton-pipelines
```

You should see output like this:

```
NAME                                          READY   STATUS    RESTARTS   AGE
tekton-pipelines-controller-5fd68749f5-tz8dv  1/1     Running   0          3m4s
tekton-pipelines-webhook-58dcdbfd9b-hswpk     1/1     Running   0          3m4s
```

> The preceding command goes in watch mode, thus it remains
> appended. Press Ctrl+C in order to stop it when you see the con-
> troller and webhook pods in Running status.

Then you can install Tekton Triggers (*https://oreil.ly/Vq32h*). At the time of writing
this book, we are using version 0.20.1:

```
kubectl apply \
-f https://storage.googleapis.com/tekton-releases/triggers/previous/v0.20.1/
release.yaml
```

You should see the following output:

```
podsecuritypolicy.policy/tekton-triggers created
clusterrole.rbac.authorization.k8s.io/tekton-triggers-admin created
clusterrole.rbac.authorization.k8s.io/tekton-triggers-core-interceptors created
clusterrole.rbac.authorization.k8s.io/tekton-triggers-core-interceptors-secrets
created
clusterrole.rbac.authorization.k8s.io/tekton-triggers-eventlistener-roles created
```

```
clusterrole.rbac.authorization.k8s.io/tekton-triggers-eventlistener-clusterroles
created
role.rbac.authorization.k8s.io/tekton-triggers-admin created
role.rbac.authorization.k8s.io/tekton-triggers-admin-webhook created
role.rbac.authorization.k8s.io/tekton-triggers-core-interceptors created
role.rbac.authorization.k8s.io/tekton-triggers-info created
serviceaccount/tekton-triggers-controller created
serviceaccount/tekton-triggers-webhook created
serviceaccount/tekton-triggers-core-interceptors created
clusterrolebinding.rbac.authorization.k8s.io/tekton-triggers-controller-admin cre-
ated
clusterrolebinding.rbac.authorization.k8s.io/tekton-triggers-webhook-admin created
clusterrolebinding.rbac.authorization.k8s.io/tekton-triggers-core-interceptors cre-
ated
clusterrolebinding.rbac.authorization.k8s.io/tekton-triggers-core-interceptors-
secrets created
rolebinding.rbac.authorization.k8s.io/tekton-triggers-controller-admin created
rolebinding.rbac.authorization.k8s.io/tekton-triggers-webhook-admin created
rolebinding.rbac.authorization.k8s.io/tekton-triggers-core-interceptors created
rolebinding.rbac.authorization.k8s.io/tekton-triggers-info created
customresourcedefinition.apiextensions.k8s.io/clusterinterceptors.triggers.tek-
ton.dev created
customresourcedefinition.apiextensions.k8s.io/clustertriggerbindings.triggers.tek-
ton.dev created
customresourcedefinition.apiextensions.k8s.io/eventlisteners.triggers.tekton.dev
created
customresourcedefinition.apiextensions.k8s.io/triggers.triggers.tekton.dev created
customresourcedefinition.apiextensions.k8s.io/triggerbindings.triggers.tekton.dev
created
customresourcedefinition.apiextensions.k8s.io/triggertemplates.triggers.tekton.dev
created
secret/triggers-webhook-certs created
validatingwebhookconfiguration.admissionregistration.k8s.io/validation.web-
hook.triggers.tekton.dev created
mutatingwebhookconfiguration.admissionregistration.k8s.io/webhook.triggers.tek-
ton.dev created
validatingwebhookconfiguration.admissionregistration.k8s.io/config.webhook.trig-
gers.tekton.dev created
clusterrole.rbac.authorization.k8s.io/tekton-triggers-aggregate-edit created
clusterrole.rbac.authorization.k8s.io/tekton-triggers-aggregate-view created
configmap/config-defaults-triggers created
configmap/feature-flags-triggers created
configmap/triggers-info created
configmap/config-logging-triggers created
configmap/config-observability-triggers created
service/tekton-triggers-controller created
deployment.apps/tekton-triggers-controller created
service/tekton-triggers-webhook created
deployment.apps/tekton-triggers-webhook created
deployment.apps/tekton-triggers-core-interceptors created
service/tekton-triggers-core-interceptors created
clusterinterceptor.triggers.tekton.dev/cel created
clusterinterceptor.triggers.tekton.dev/bitbucket created
clusterinterceptor.triggers.tekton.dev/github created
```

```
clusterinterceptor.triggers.tekton.dev/gitlab created
secret/tekton-triggers-core-interceptors-certs created
```

You can monitor and verify the installation with the following command:

```
kubectl get pods -w -n tekton-pipelines
```

You should see three new pods created and running—`tekton-triggers-controller`, `tekton-triggers-core-interceptors`, and `tekton-triggers-webhook`:

```
NAME                                              READY   STATUS    RESTARTS
AGE
tekton-pipelines-controller-5fd68749f5-tz8dv      1/1     Running   0
27m
tekton-pipelines-webhook-58dcdbfd9b-hswpk         1/1     Running   0
27m
tekton-triggers-controller-854d44fd5d-8jf9q       1/1     Running   0
105s
tekton-triggers-core-interceptors-5454f8785f-dhsrb 1/1    Running   0
104s
tekton-triggers-webhook-86d75f875-zmjf4           1/1     Running   0
105s
```

After this you have a fully working Tekton installation on top of your Kubernetes cluster, supporting Pipelines and automation via event Triggers. In addition to that, you could install the Tekton Dashboard (*https://oreil.ly/Db56q*) in order to visualize Tasks, Pipelines, and logs via a nice UI. At the time of writing this book, we are using version 0.28.0:

```
kubectl apply \
-f https://storage.googleapis.com/tekton-releases/dashboard/previous/v0.28.0/
tekton-dashboard-release.yaml
```

You should have output similar to the following:

```
customresourcedefinition.apiextensions.k8s.io/extensions.dashboard.tekton.dev cre-
ated
serviceaccount/tekton-dashboard created
role.rbac.authorization.k8s.io/tekton-dashboard-info created
clusterrole.rbac.authorization.k8s.io/tekton-dashboard-backend created
clusterrole.rbac.authorization.k8s.io/tekton-dashboard-tenant created
rolebinding.rbac.authorization.k8s.io/tekton-dashboard-info created
clusterrolebinding.rbac.authorization.k8s.io/tekton-dashboard-backend created
configmap/dashboard-info created
service/tekton-dashboard created
deployment.apps/tekton-dashboard created
clusterrolebinding.rbac.authorization.k8s.io/tekton-dashboard-tenant created
```

You can monitor and verify the installation with the following command:

```
kubectl get pods -w -n tekton-pipelines
```

You should see a new pod created and running—`tekton-dashboard`:

```
NAME                                             READY  STATUS   RESTARTS
AGE
tekton-dashboard-786b6b5579-sscgz                1/1    Running  0
2m25s
tekton-pipelines-controller-5fd68749f5-tz8dv     1/1    Running  1 (7m16s ago)
5d7h
tekton-pipelines-webhook-58dcdbfd9b-hswpk        1/1    Running  1 (7m6s ago)
5d7h
tekton-triggers-controller-854d44fd5d-8jf9q      1/1    Running  2 (7m9s ago)
5d7h
tekton-triggers-core-interceptors-5454f8785f-dhsrb  1/1  Running  1 (7m7s ago)
5d7h
tekton-triggers-webhook-86d75f875-zmjf4          1/1    Running  2 (7m9s ago)
5d7h
```

By default, the Dashboard is not exposed outside the Kubernetes cluster. You can access it by using the following command:

```
kubectl port-forward svc/tekton-dashboard 9097:9097 -n tekton-pipelines
```

 There are several ways to expose internal services in Kubernetes; you could also create an Ingress (*https://oreil.ly/wwWcX*) for that as shown in the Tekton Dashboard documentation (*https://oreil.ly/BeOlq*).

You can now browse to *http://localhost:9097* to access your Dashboard, as shown in Figure 6-2.

You can download and install the Tekton CLI (*https://oreil.ly/U7FSt*) for your OS to start creating Tasks and Pipelines from the command line. At the time of writing this book, we are using version 0.25.0.

Figure 6-2. Tekton Dashboard

Finally, verify that tkn and Tekton are configured correctly:

```
tkn version
```

You should get the following output:

```
Client version: 0.25.0
Pipeline version: v0.37.0
Triggers version: v0.20.1
Dashboard version: v0.28.0
```

See Also

- Tekton Getting Started (*https://oreil.ly/7I7ev*)

6.2 Create a Hello World Task

Problem

You want to start using Tekton by exploring Tasks and creating a sample one.

Solution

In Tekton, a Task defines a series of steps that run sequentially to perform logic that the Task requires. Every Task (*https://oreil.ly/5ldpn*) runs as a pod on your Kubernetes cluster, with each step running in its own container. While steps within a Task are sequential, Tasks can be executed inside a Pipeline in parallel. Therefore, Tasks are the building blocks for running Pipelines with Tekton.

Let's create a Hello World Task:

```
apiVersion: tekton.dev/v1beta1
kind: Task ❶
metadata:
  name: hello ❷
spec:
  steps: ❸
    - name: say-hello ❹
      image: registry.access.redhat.com/ubi8/ubi ❺
      command:
        - /bin/bash
      args: ['-c', 'echo Hello GitOps Cookbook reader!']
```

❶ The API as an object of kind Task

❷ The name of the Task

❸ The list of steps contained within this Task, in this case just one

❹ The name of the step

❺ The container image where the step starts

First you need to create this resource in Kubernetes:

```
kubectl create -f helloworld-task.yaml
```

You should get the following output:

```
task.tekton.dev/hello created
```

You can verify that the object has been created in your current Kubernetes namespace:

```
kubectl get tasks
```

You should get output similar to the following:

```
NAME    AGE
hello   90s
```

Now you can start your Tekton Task with `tkn` CLI:

```
tkn task start --showlog hello
```

You should get output similar to the following:

```
TaskRun started: hello-run-8bmzz
Waiting for logs to be available...
[say-hello] Hello World
```

 A TaskRun is the API representation of a running Task. See Recipe 6.3 for more details.

See Also

- Tekton Task documentation (*https://oreil.ly/5ldpn*)

6.3 Create a Task to Compile and Package an App from Git

Problem

You want to automate compiling and packaging an app from Git on Kubernetes with Tekton.

Solution

As seen in Recipe 6.2, Tekton Tasks have a flexible mechanism to add a list of sequential steps to automate actions. The idea is to create a list of Tasks with a chain of input/output that can be used to compose Pipelines. Therefore a Task can contain a series of optional fields for a better control over the resource:

inputs
> The resources ingested by the Task.

outputs
> The resources produced by the Task.

params
> The parameters that will be used in the Task steps. Each parameter has:

> name
>> The name of the parameter.

> description
>> The description of the parameter.

> default
>> The default value of the parameter.

> results
>> The names under which Tasks write execution results.

> workspaces
>> The paths to volumes needed by the Task.

> volumes
>> The Task can also mount external volumes using the volumes attribute.

The following example, as illustrated in Figure 6-3, shows a Task named build-app that clones the sources using the git command and lists the source code in output.

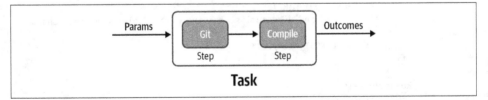

Figure 6-3. build-app Task

```
apiVersion: tekton.dev/v1beta1
kind: Task
metadata:
  name: build-app
```

```
spec:
  workspaces: ❶
    - name: source
      description: The git repo will be cloned onto the volume backing this work
space
  params: ❷
    - name: contextDir
      description: the context dir within source
      default: quarkus
    - name: tlsVerify
      description: tls verify
      type: string
      default: "false"
    - name: url
      default: https://github.com/gitops-cookbook/tekton-tutorial-greeter.git
    - name: revision
      default: master
    - name: subdirectory
      default: ""
    - name: sslVerify
      description: defines if http.sslVerify should be set to true or false in the
global git config
      type: string
      default: "false"
  steps:
    - image: 'gcr.io/tekton-releases/github.com/tektoncd/pipeline/cmd/git-
init:v0.21.0'
      name: clone
      resources: {}
      script: |
        CHECKOUT_DIR="$(workspaces.source.path)/$(params.subdirectory)"
        cleandir() {
          # Delete any existing contents of the repo directory if it exists.
          #
          # We don't just "rm -rf $CHECKOUT_DIR" because $CHECKOUT_DIR might be "/"
          # or the root of a mounted volume.
          if [[ -d "$CHECKOUT_DIR" ]] ; then
            # Delete non-hidden files and directories
            rm -rf "$CHECKOUT_DIR"/*
            # Delete files and directories starting with . but excluding ..
            rm -rf "$CHECKOUT_DIR"/.[!.]*
            # Delete files and directories starting with .. plus any other charac
ter
            rm -rf "$CHECKOUT_DIR"/..?*
          fi
        }
        /ko-app/git-init \
          -url "$(params.url)" \
          -revision "$(params.revision)" \
          -path "$CHECKOUT_DIR" \
          -sslVerify="$(params.sslVerify)"
        cd "$CHECKOUT_DIR"
        RESULT_SHA="$(git rev-parse HEAD)"
    - name: build-sources
```

```
image: gcr.io/cloud-builders/mvn
command:
  - mvn
args:
  - -DskipTests
  - clean
  - install
env:
  - name: user.home
    value: /home/tekton
workingDir: "/workspace/source/$(params.contextDir)"
```

❶ A Task step and Pipeline Task can share a common filesystem via a Tekton workspace. The workspace could be either backed by something like Persistent-VolumeClaim (PVC) and a ConfigMap, or just ephemeral (emptyDir).

❷ A Task can have parameters; this feature makes the execution dynamic.

Let's create the Task with the following command:

```
kubectl create -f build-app-task.yaml
```

You should get output similar to the following:

```
task.tekton.dev/build-app created
```

You can verify that the object has been created in your current Kubernetes namespace:

```
kubectl get tasks
```

You should get output similar to the following:

```
NAME        AGE
build-app   3s
```

You can also list the Task with the tkn CLI:

```
tkn task ls
```

You should get output similar to the following:

```
NAME        DESCRIPTION   AGE
build-app                 10 seconds ago
```

When you start a Task, a new TaskRun (*https://oreil.ly/MZ5DY*) object is created. TaskRuns are the API representation of a running Task; thus you can create it with the tkn CLI using the following command:

```
tkn task start build-app \
  --param contextDir='quarkus' \
  --workspace name=source,emptyDir="" \
  --showlog
```

When parameters are used inside a Task or Pipeline, you will be prompted to add new values or confirm default ones, if any. In order to use the default values from the Task defintion without prompting for values, you can use the `--use-param-defaults` option.

You should get output similar to the following:

```
? Value for param `tlsVerify` of type `string`? (Default is `false`) false
? Value for param `url` of type `string`? (Default is `https://
github.com/gitops-cookbook/tekton-tutorial-greeter.git`) https://github.com/gitops-
cookbook/tekton-tutorial-greeter.git
? Value for param `revision` of type `string`? (Default is `master`) master
? Value for param `subdirectory` of type `string`? (Default is ``)
? Value for param `sslVerify` of type `string`? (Default is `false`) false
TaskRun started: build-app-run-rzcd8
Waiting for logs to be available...
[clone] {"level":"info","ts":1659278019.0018234,"caller":"git/
git.go:169","msg":"Successfully cloned https://github.com/gitops-cookbook/tekton-
tutorial-greeter.git @ d9291c456db1ce29177b77ffeaa9b71ad80a50e6 (grafted, HEAD, ori
gin/master) in path /workspace/source/"}
[clone] {"level":"info","ts":1659278019.0227938,"caller":"git/
git.go:207","msg":"Successfully initialized and updated submodules in path /work
space/source/"}

[build-sources] [INFO] Scanning for projects...
[build-sources] Downloading from central: https://repo.maven.apache.org/maven2/io/
quarkus/quarkus-universe-bom/1.6.1.Final/quarkus-universe-bom-1.6.1.Final.pom
Downloaded from central: https://repo.maven.apache.org/maven2/io/quarkus/quarkus-
universe-bom/1.6.1.Final/quarkus-universe-bom-1.6.1.Final.pom (412 kB at 118 kB/s)
[build-sources] [INFO]
...
[build-sources] [INFO] Installing /workspace/source/quarkus/target/tekton-quarkus-
greeter.jar to /root/.m2/repository/com/redhat/developers/tekton-quarkus-greeter/
1.0.0-SNAPSHOT/tekton-quarkus-greeter-1.0.0-SNAPSHOT.jar
[build-sources] [INFO] Installing /workspace/source/quar-
kus/pom.xml to /root/.m2/repository/com/redhat/developers/tekton-quarkus-greeter/
1.0.0-SNAPSHOT/tekton-quarkus-greeter-1.0.0-SNAPSHOT.pom
[build-sources] [INFO]
-------------------------------------------------------------------------
[build-sources] [INFO] BUILD SUCCESS
[build-sources] [INFO]
-------------------------------------------------------------------------
[build-sources] [INFO] Total time:  04:41 min
[build-sources] [INFO] Finished at: 2022-07-31T14:38:22Z
[build-sources] [INFO]
-------------------------------------------------------------------------
```

Or, you can create a `TaskRun` object manually like this:

```
apiVersion: tekton.dev/v1beta1
kind: TaskRun
metadata:
```

```
    generateName: build-app-run- ❶
    labels:
      app.kubernetes.io/managed-by: tekton-pipelines
      tekton.dev/task: build-app
spec:
  params:
  - name: contextDir
    value: quarkus
  - name: revision
    value: master
  - name: sslVerify
    value: "false"
  - name: subdirectory
    value: ""
  - name: tlsVerify
    value: "false"
  - name: url
    value: https://github.com/gitops-cookbook/tekton-tutorial-greeter.git
  taskRef: ❷
    kind: Task
    name: build-app
  workspaces:
  - emptyDir: {}
    name: source
```

❶ If you don't want to specify a name for each TaskRun, you can use the generate
   Name attribute to let Tekton pick a random one from the string you defined.

❷ Here you list the Task that the TaskRun is referring to.

And start it in this way:

```
kubectl create -f build-app-taskrun.yaml
```

You should get output similar to the following:

```
taskrun.tekton.dev/build-app-run-65vmh created
```

You can also verify it with the tkn CLI:

```
tkn taskrun ls
```

You should get output similar to the following:

```
NAME                 STARTED         DURATION   STATUS
build-app-run-65vmh  1 minutes ago   2m37s      Succeeded
build-app-run-rzcd8  2 minutes ago   3m58s      Succeeded
```

You can get the logs from the TaskRun by specifying the name of the TaskRun:

```
tkn taskrun logs build-app-run-65vmh -f
```

See Also

Debugging a TaskRun (*https://oreil.ly/PxRNG*)

6.4 Create a Task to Compile and Package an App from Private Git

Problem

You want to use a private Git repository to automate compiling and packaging of an app on Kubernetes with Tekton.

Solution

In Recipe 6.3 you saw how to compile and package a sample Java application using a public Git repository, but most of the time people deal with private repos at work, so how do you integrate them? Tekton supports the following authentication schemes for use with Git:

- Basic-auth
- SSH

With both options you can use a Kubernetes Secret (*https://oreil.ly/Oxj6W*) to store your credentials and attach them to the `ServiceAccount` (*https://oreil.ly/6UC3O*) running your Tekton Tasks or Pipelines.

Tekton uses a default service account, however you can override it following the documentation here (*https://oreil.ly/ID6m0*).

Let's start with a common example of basic authentication and a popular Git service such as GitHub.

GitHub uses personal access tokens (PATs) as an alternative to using passwords for authentication. You can use a PAT instead of a clear-text password to enhance security.

First you need to create a Secret. You can do this by creating the following YAML file:

```
apiVersion: v1
kind: Secret
metadata:
  name: github-secret
  annotations:
    tekton.dev/git-0: https://github.com ❶
type: kubernetes.io/basic-auth ❷
stringData:
  username: YOUR_USERNAME ❸
  password: YOUR_PASSWORD ❹
```

❶ Here you specify the URL for which Tekton will use this Secret, in this case GitHub

❷ This is the type of Secret, in this case a basic authentication one

❸ Your Git user, in this case your GitHub user

❹ You Git password, in this case your GitHub personal access token

You can now create the Secret with the following command:

```
kubectl create -f git-secret.yaml
```

You should get the following output:

```
secret/git-secret created
```

You can also avoid writing YAML and do everything with kubectl as follows:

```
kubectl create secret generic git-secret \
    --type=kubernetes.io/basic-auth \
    --from-literal=username=YOUR_USERNAME \
    --from-literal=password=YOUR_PASSWORD
```

And then you just annotate the Secret as follows:

```
kubectl annotate secret git-secret "tekton.dev/git-0=https://github.com"
```

Once you have created and annotated your Secret, you have to attach it to the ServiceAccount running your Tekton Tasks or Pipelines.

Let's create a new ServiceAccount for this purpose:

```
apiVersion: v1
kind: ServiceAccount
metadata:
  name: tekton-bot-sa
secrets:
  - name: git-secret ❶
```

❶ List of Secrets attached to this ServiceAccount

```
kubectl create -f tekton-bot-sa.yaml
```

You should get the following output:

```
serviceaccount/tekton-bot-sa created
```

 You can create the ServiceAccount directly with kubectl as
follows:

```
kubectl create serviceaccount tekton-bot-sa
```

and then patch it to add the secret reference:

```
kubectl patch serviceaccount tekton-bot-sa -p
'{"secrets": [{"name": "git-secret"}]}'
```

Once credentials are set up and linked to the ServiceAccount running Tasks or Pipelines, you can just add the --serviceaccount=<NAME> option to your tkn command, using the Recipe 6.3 example:

```
tkn task start build-app \
  --serviceaccount='tekton-bot-sa' \ ❶
  --param url='https://github.com/gitops-cookbook/tekton-greeter-private.git' \ ❷
  --param contextDir='quarkus' \
  --workspace name=source,emptyDir="" \
  --showlog
```

❶ Here you specify the ServiceAccount to use; this will override the default one at runtime.

❷ Here you can override the default repository with one of your choice. In this example there's a private repository that you cannot access, but you can create a private repository on your own and test it like this.

You should get output similar to the following:

```
...
[clone] {"level":"info","ts":1659354692.1365478,"caller":"git/
git.go:169","msg":"Successfully cloned https://github.com/gitops-cookbook/tekton-
greeter-private.git @ 5250e1fa185805373e620d1c04a0c48129efd2ee (grafted, HEAD, ori
gin/master) in path /workspace/source/"}
[clone] {"level":"info","ts":1659354692.1546066,"caller":"git/
git.go:207","msg":"Successfully initialized and updated submodules in path /work
space/source/"}
...
[build-sources] [INFO]
-------------------------------------------------------------------
[build-sources] [INFO] BUILD SUCCESS
[build-sources] [INFO]
-------------------------------------------------------------------
[build-sources] [INFO] Total time:  04:30 min
[build-sources] [INFO] Finished at: 2022-07-31T15:30:01Z
```

```
[build-sources] [INFO]
```

See Also

- Tekton Authentication (*https://oreil.ly/6W9xF*)

6.5 Containerize an Application Using a Tekton Task and Buildah

Problem

You want to compile, package, and containerize your app with a Tekton Task on Kubernetes.

Solution

Automation is essential when adopting the cloud native approach, and if you decide to use Kubernetes for your CI/CD workloads, you need to provide a way to package and deploy your applications.

In fact, Kubernetes per se doesn't have a built-in mechanism to build containers; it just relies on add-ons such as Tekton or external services for this purpose. That's why in Chapter 3 we did an overview on how to create containers for packaging applications with various open source tools. In Recipe 3.3 we used Buildah to create a container from a Dockerfile.

Thanks to Tekton's extensible model, you can reuse the same Task defined in Recipe 6.3 to add a step to create a container using the outcomes from the previous steps, as shown in Figure 6-4.

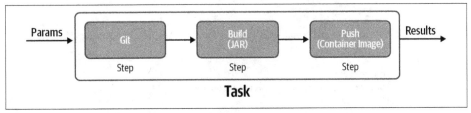

Figure 6-4. Build Push app

The container can be pushed to a public container registry such as DockerHub or Quay.io, or to a private container registry. Similar to what we have seen in Recipe 6.4 for private Git repositories, pushing a container image to a container registry needs authentication. A Secret needs to be attached to the `ServiceAccount` running the Task as follows. See Chapter 2 for how to register and use a public registry.

```
kubectl create secret docker-registry container-registry-secret \
  --docker-server='YOUR_REGISTRY_SERVER' \
  --docker-username='YOUR_REGISTRY_USER' \
  --docker-password='YOUR_REGISTRY_PASS'
```

```
secret/container-registry-secret created
```

Verify it is present and check that the Secret is of type kubernetes.io/dockercon
figjson:

```
kubectl get secrets
```

You should get the following output:

```
NAME                         TYPE                               DATA   AGE
container-registry-secret    kubernetes.io/dockerconfigjson     1      1s
```

Let's create a ServiceAccount for this Task:

```
kubectl create serviceaccount tekton-registry-sa
```

Then let's add the previously generated Secret to this ServiceAccount:

```
kubectl patch serviceaccount tekton-registry-sa \
  -p '{"secrets": [{"name": "container-registry-secret"}]}'
```

You should get the following output:

```
serviceaccount/tekton-registry-sa patched
```

Let's add a new step to create a container image and push it to a container registry.
In the following example we use the book's organization repos at Quay.io—quay.io/
gitops-cookbook/tekton-greeter:latest:

```
apiVersion: tekton.dev/v1beta1
kind: Task
metadata:
  name: build-push-app
spec:
  workspaces:
    - name: source
      description: The git repo will be cloned onto the volume backing this work
space
  params:
    - name: contextDir
      description: the context dir within source
      default: quarkus
    - name: tlsVerify
      description: tls verify
      type: string
      default: "false"
    - name: url
      default: https://github.com/gitops-cookbook/tekton-tutorial-greeter.git
    - name: revision
      default: master
    - name: subdirectory
```

```
          default: ""
      - name: sslVerify
        description: defines if http.sslVerify should be set to true or false in the
global git config
        type: string
        default: "false"
      - name: storageDriver
        type: string
        description: Storage driver
        default: vfs
      - name: destinationImage
        description: the fully qualified image name
        default: ""
  steps:
    - image: 'gcr.io/tekton-releases/github.com/tektoncd/pipeline/cmd/git-
init:v0.21.0'
      name: clone
      resources: {}
      script: |
        CHECKOUT_DIR="$(workspaces.source.path)/$(params.subdirectory)"
        cleandir() {
          # Delete any existing contents of the repo directory if it exists.
          #
          # We don't just "rm -rf $CHECKOUT_DIR" because $CHECKOUT_DIR might be "/"
          # or the root of a mounted volume.
          if [[ -d "$CHECKOUT_DIR" ]] ; then
            # Delete non-hidden files and directories
            rm -rf "$CHECKOUT_DIR"/*
            # Delete files and directories starting with . but excluding ..
            rm -rf "$CHECKOUT_DIR"/.[!.]*
            # Delete files and directories starting with .. plus any other charac
ter
            rm -rf "$CHECKOUT_DIR"/..?*
          fi
        }
        /ko-app/git-init \
          -url "$(params.url)" \
          -revision "$(params.revision)" \
          -path "$CHECKOUT_DIR" \
          -sslVerify="$(params.sslVerify)"
        cd "$CHECKOUT_DIR"
        RESULT_SHA="$(git rev-parse HEAD)"
    - name: build-sources
      image: gcr.io/cloud-builders/mvn
      command:
        - mvn
      args:
        - -DskipTests
        - clean
        - install
      env:
        - name: user.home
          value: /home/tekton
      workingDir: "/workspace/source/$(params.contextDir)"
```

```
  - name: build-and-push-image
    image: quay.io/buildah/stable
    script: |
      #!/usr/bin/env bash
      buildah --storage-driver=$STORAGE_DRIVER --tls-verify=$(params.tlsVerify)
bud --layers -t $DESTINATION_IMAGE $CONTEXT_DIR
      buildah --storage-driver=$STORAGE_DRIVER --tls-verify=$(params.tlsVerify)
push $DESTINATION_IMAGE docker://$DESTINATION_IMAGE
    env:
      - name: DESTINATION_IMAGE
        value: "$(params.destinationImage)"
      - name: CONTEXT_DIR
        value: "/workspace/source/$(params.contextDir)"
      - name: STORAGE_DRIVER
        value: "$(params.storageDriver)"
    workingDir: "/workspace/source/$(params.contextDir)"
    volumeMounts:
      - name: varlibc
        mountPath: /var/lib/containers
volumes:
  - name: varlibc
    emptyDir: {}
```

Let's create this Task:

```
kubectl create -f build-push-app.yaml
```

You should get the following output:

```
task.tekton.dev/build-push-app created
```

Now let's start the Task with the Buildah step creating a container image and with a new parameter destinationImage to specify where to push the resulting container image:

```
tkn task start build-push-app \
  --serviceaccount='tekton-registry-sa' \
  --param url='https://github.com/gitops-cookbook/tekton-tutorial-greeter.git' \
  --param destinationImage='quay.io/gitops-cookbook/tekton-greeter:latest' \  ❶
  --param contextDir='quarkus' \
  --workspace name=source,emptyDir="" \
  --use-param-defaults \
  --showlog
```

 Here you can place your registry; in this example we are using the book's organization repos at Quay.io.

You should get output similar to the following:

```
...
Downloaded from central: https://repo.maven.apache.org/maven2/org/codehaus/plexus/
plexus-utils/3.0.5/plexus-utils-3.0.5.jar (230 kB at 301 kB/s)
[build-sources] [INFO] Installing /workspace/source/quarkus/target/tekton-quarkus-
greeter.jar to /root/.m2/repository/com/redhat/developers/tekton-quarkus-greeter/
1.0.0-SNAPSHOT/tekton-quarkus-greeter-1.0.0-SNAPSHOT.jar
```

```
[build-sources] [INFO] Installing /workspace/source/quar-
kus/pom.xml to /root/.m2/repository/com/redhat/developers/tekton-quarkus-greeter/
1.0.0-SNAPSHOT/tekton-quarkus-greeter-1.0.0-SNAPSHOT.pom
[build-sources] [INFO]
------------------------------------------------------------------------
[build-sources] [INFO] BUILD SUCCESS
[build-sources] [INFO]
------------------------------------------------------------------------
[build-sources] [INFO] Total time:  02:59 min
[build-sources] [INFO] Finished at: 2022-08-02T06:18:37Z
[build-sources] [INFO]
------------------------------------------------------------------------
[build-and-push-image] STEP 1/2: FROM registry.access.redhat.com/ubi8/openjdk-11
[build-and-push-image] Trying to pull registry.access.redhat.com/ubi8/
openjdk-11:latest...
[build-and-push-image] Getting image source signatures
[build-and-push-image] Checking if image destination supports signatures
[build-and-push-image] Copying blob
sha256:1e09a5ee0038fbe06a18e7f355188bbabc387467144abcd435f7544fef395aa1
[build-and-push-image] Copying blob
sha256:0d725b91398ed3db11249808d89e688e62e511bbd4a2e875ed8493ce1febdb2c
[build-and-push-image] Copying blob
sha256:1e09a5ee0038fbe06a18e7f355188bbabc387467144abcd435f7544fef395aa1
[build-and-push-image] Copying blob
sha256:0d725b91398ed3db11249808d89e688e62e511bbd4a2e875ed8493ce1febdb2c
[build-and-push-image] Copying blob
sha256:e441d34134fac91baa79be3e2bb8fb3dba71ba5c1ea012cb5daeb7180a054687
[build-and-push-image] Copying blob
sha256:e441d34134fac91baa79be3e2bb8fb3dba71ba5c1ea012cb5daeb7180a054687
[build-and-push-image] Copying config
sha256:0c308464b19eaa9a01c3fdd6b63a043c160d4eea85e461bbbb7d01d168f6d993
[build-and-push-image] Writing manifest to image destination
[build-and-push-image] Storing signatures
[build-and-push-image] STEP 2/2: COPY target/quarkus-app /deployments/
[build-and-push-image] COMMIT quay.io/gitops-cookbook/tekton-greeter:latest
[build-and-push-image] --> 42fe38b4346
[build-and-push-image] Successfully tagged quay.io/gitops-cookbook/tekton-
greeter:latest
[build-and-push-image]
42fe38b43468c3ca32262dbea6fd78919aba2bd35981cd4f71391e07786c9e21
[build-and-push-image] Getting image source signatures
[build-and-push-image] Copying blob
sha256:647a854c512bad44709221b6b0973e884f29bcb5a380ee32e95bfb0189b620e6
[build-and-push-image] Copying blob
sha256:f2ee6b2834726167d0de06f3bbe65962aef79855c5ede0d2ba93b4408558d9c9
[build-and-push-image] Copying blob
sha256:8e0e04b5c700a86f4a112f41e7e767a9d7c539fe3391611313bf76edb07eeab1
[build-and-push-image] Copying blob
sha256:69c55192bed92cbb669c88eb3c36449b64ac93ae466abfff2a575273ce05a39e
[build-and-push-image] Copying config
sha256:42fe38b43468c3ca32262dbea6fd78919aba2bd35981cd4f71391e07786c9e21
[build-and-push-image] Writing manifest to image destination
[build-and-push-image] Storing signatures
```

See Also

- Buildah (*https://buildah.io*)
- Docker Authentication for Tekton (*https://oreil.ly/QJlVW*)

6.6 Deploy an Application to Kubernetes Using a Tekton Task

Problem

You want to deploy an application from a container image to Kubernetes with a Tekton Task.

Solution

While in Recipes 6.3, 6.4, and 6.5 we have listed a Tekton Task that is useful for continuous integration (CI), in this recipe we'll start having a look at the Continous Deployment (CD) part by deploying an existing container image to Kubernetes.

We can reuse the container image we created and pushed in Recipe 6.5, available at quay.io/gitops-cookbook/tekton-greeter:latest:

```
apiVersion: tekton.dev/v1beta1
kind: Task
metadata:
  name: kubectl
spec:
  params:
    - name: SCRIPT
      description: The kubectl CLI arguments to run
      type: string
      default: "kubectl help"
  steps:
    - name: oc
      image: quay.io/openshift/origin-cli:latest 
      script: |
        #!/usr/bin/env bash

        $(params.SCRIPT)
```

 For this example we are using kubectl from this container image, which also contains OpenShift CLI and it has an smaller size compared to gcr.io/cloud-builders/kubectl.

Let's create this Task:

```
kubectl create -f kubectl-task.yaml
```

You should get the following output:

```
task.tekton.dev/kubectl created
```

As discussed in Recipe 6.5, Tekton uses a default `ServiceAccount` for running Tasks and Pipelines, unless a specific one is defined at runtime or overridden at a global scope. The best practice is always to create a specific `ServiceAccount` for a particular action, so let's create one named `tekton-deployer-sa` for this use case as follows:

```
kubectl create serviceaccount tekton-deployer-sa
```

You should get the following output:

```
serviceaccount/tekton-deployer-sa created
```

A `ServiceAccount` needs permission to deploy an application to Kubernetes. Roles and RoleBindings (*https://oreil.ly/6ov6J*) are API objects used to map a certain permission to a user or a `ServiceAccount`.

You first define a Role named `pipeline-role` for the `ServiceAccount` running the Tekton Task with permissions to deploy apps:

```
apiVersion: rbac.authorization.k8s.io/v1
kind: Role
metadata:
  name: task-role
rules:
  - apiGroups:
      - ""
    resources:
      - pods
      - services
      - endpoints
      - configmaps
      - secrets
    verbs:
      - "*"
  - apiGroups:
      - apps
    resources:
      - deployments
      - replicasets
    verbs:
      - "*"
  - apiGroups:
      - ""
    resources:
      - pods
    verbs:
      - get
  - apiGroups:
      - apps
    resources:
      - replicasets
```

```
verbs:
  - get
```

Now you need to bind the Role to the `ServiceAccount`:

```
apiVersion: rbac.authorization.k8s.io/v1
kind: RoleBinding
metadata:
  name: task-role-binding
roleRef:
  kind: Role
  name: task-role
  apiGroup: rbac.authorization.k8s.io
subjects:
  - kind: ServiceAccount
    name: tekton-deployer-sa
```

Now you can create the two resources as follows:

```
kubectl create -f task-role.yaml
kubectl create -f task-role-binding.yaml
```

You should get the following output:

```
role.rbac.authorization.k8s.io/task-role created
rolebinding.rbac.authorization.k8s.io/task-role-binding created
```

Finally, you can define a TaskRun as follows:

```
apiVersion: tekton.dev/v1beta1
kind: TaskRun
metadata:
  name: kubectl-taskrun
spec:
  serviceAccountName: tekton-deployer-sa
  taskRef:
    name: kubectl
  params:
    - name: SCRIPT
      value: |
        kubectl create deploy tekton-greeter --image=quay.io/gitops-cookbook/
tekton-greeter:latest
```

And run it in this way:

```
kubectl create -f kubectl-taskrun.yaml
```

You should get the following output:

```
taskrun.tekton.dev/kubectl-run created
```

You can check the logs to see the results:

```
tkn taskrun logs kubectl-run -f
```

You should get output similar to the following:

```
? Select taskrun: kubectl-run started 9 seconds ago
[oc] deployment.apps/tekton-greeter created
```

After a few seconds you should see the Deployment in Ready state:

```
kubectl get deploy
```

```
NAME              READY   UP-TO-DATE   AVAILABLE   AGE
tekton-greeter    1/1     1            0           30s
```

 The first time might take a while due to the time it takes to pull the container image.

Check if the app is available, expose the Deployment, and forward Kubernetes traffic to your workstation to test it:

```
kubectl expose deploy/tekton-greeter --port 8080
kubectl port-forward svc/tekton-greeter 8080:8080
```

In another terminal, run this command:

```
curl localhost:8080
```

You should see the following output:

```
Meeow!! from Tekton ----
```

See Also

- Tekton Task (*https://oreil.ly/YlIZI*)

6.7 Create a Tekton Pipeline to Build and Deploy an App to Kubernetes

Problem

You want to create a Pipeline to compile, package, and deploy an app on Kubernetes with Tekton.

Solution

In the previous recipes we have seen how to create Tasks to execute one or more steps sequentially to build apps. In this recipe we will discuss Tekton Pipelines (*https://oreil.ly/aN8lv*), a collection of Tasks that you can define and compose in a specific order of execution, either sequentially or in parallel, as you can see in Figure 6-5.

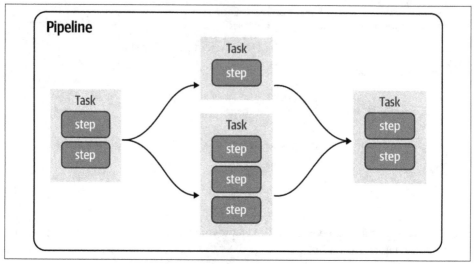

Figure 6-5. Tekton Pipelines flows

Tekton Pipelines supports parameters and a mechanism to exchange outcomes between different Tasks. For instance, using the examples shown in Recipes 6.5 and 6.6:

```
kubectl patch serviceaccount tekton-deployer-sa \
  -p '{"secrets": [{"name": "container-registry-secret"}]}'

apiVersion: tekton.dev/v1beta1
kind: Pipeline
metadata:
  name: tekton-greeter-pipeline
spec:
  params: ❶
    - name: GIT_REPO
      type: string
    - name: GIT_REF
      type: string
    - name : DESTINATION_IMAGE
      type: string
    - name : SCRIPT
      type: string
  tasks: ❷
    - name: build-push-app
      taskRef: ❸
        name: build-push-app
      params:
        - name: url
          value: "$(params.GIT_REPO)"
        - name: revision
          value: "$(params.GIT_REF)"
        - name: destinationImage
          value: "$(params.DESTINATION_IMAGE)"
```

```
      workspaces:
        - name: source
  - name: deploy-app
    taskRef:
      name: kubectl
    params:
      - name: SCRIPT
        value: "$(params.SCRIPT)"
    workspaces:
      - name: source
    runAfter: ❹
      - build-push-app
  workspaces: ❺
    - name: source
```

❶ Pipeline parameters

❷ A list of Tasks for the Pipeline

❸ The exact name of the Task to use

❹ You can decide the order with the `runAfter` field to indicate that a Task must execute after one or more other Tasks

❺ One or more common Workspaces used to share data between Tasks

Let's create the Pipeline as follows:

```
kubectl create -f tekton-greeter-pipeline.yaml
```

You should get the following output:

```
pipeline.tekton.dev/tekton-greeter-pipeline created
```

Similarly to TaskRuns, you can run this Pipeline by creating a PipelineRun (*https://oreil.ly/N8K3a*) resource as follows:

```
apiVersion: tekton.dev/v1beta1
kind: PipelineRun
metadata:
  generateName: tekton-greeter-pipeline-run-
spec:
  params:
  - name: GIT_REPO
    value: https://github.com/gitops-cookbook/tekton-tutorial-greeter.git
  - name: GIT_REF
    value: "master"
  - name: DESTINATION_IMAGE
    value: "quay.io/gitops-cookbook/tekton-greeter:latest"
  - name: SCRIPT
    value: |
        kubectl create deploy tekton-greeter --image=quay.io/gitops-cookbook/
tekton-greeter:latest
```

```
    pipelineRef:
      name: tekton-greeter-pipeline
    workspaces:
      - name: source
        emptyDir: {}
```

You can run the Pipeline by creating this PipelineRun object as follows:

```
kubectl create -f tekton-greeter-pipelinerun.yaml
```

You can check the status:

```
tkn pipelinerun ls

NAME                                 STARTED         DURATION    STATUS
tekton-greeter-pipeline-run-ntl5r    7 seconds ago   - - -       Running
```

Now that you have seen how to reuse existing Tasks within a Pipeline, it's a good time to introduce the Tekton Hub (*https://hub.tekton.dev*), a web-based platform for developers to discover, share, and contribute Tasks and Pipelines for Tekton (see Figure 6-6).

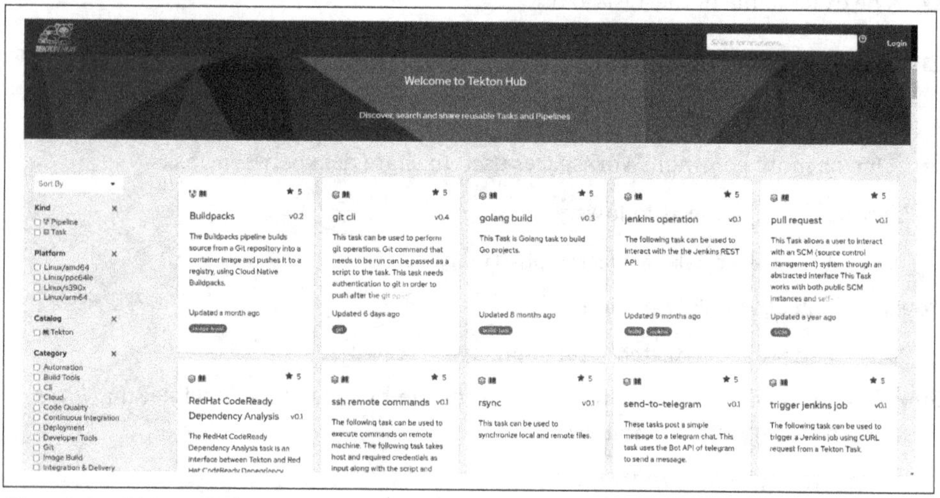

Figure 6-6. Tekton Hub

You can implement the same Pipeline with Tasks already available in the Hub. In our case, we have:

git-clone *(https://oreil.ly/tVLAG)*
: Task that clones a repo from the provided URL into the output Workspace.

buildah *(https://oreil.ly/nTUkZ)*
: Task that builds source into a container image and can push it to a container registry.

`kubernetes-actions` *(https://oreil.ly/A3Hui)*

The generic `kubectl` CLI task, which can be used to run all kinds of k8s commands.

First let's add them to our namespace as follows:

```
tkn hub install task git-clone
tkn hub install task maven
tkn hub install task buildah
tkn hub install task kubernetes-actions
```

You should get output similar to the following to confirm they are installed properly in your namespace:

```
Task git-clone(0.7) installed in default namespace
Task maven(0.2) installed in default namespace
Task buildah(0.4) installed in default namespace
Task kubernetes-actions(0.2) installed in default namespace
```

You can cross-check it with the following command:

```
kubectl get tasks
```

You should get output similar to the following:

```
NAME                 AGE
...
buildah              50s
git-clone            52s
kubernetes-actions   49s
maven                51s
...
```

 Some Tekton installations like the one made with the Operator for OpenShift Pipelines (*https://oreil.ly/dAKhL*) provide a common list of useful Tasks such as those just listed, provided as ClusterTasks. ClusterTasks are Tasks available for all namespaces within the Kubernetes cluster. Check if your installation already provides some with this command: `kubectl get clustertasks`.

Now the Pipeline has four Tasks, as you can see in Figure 6-7.

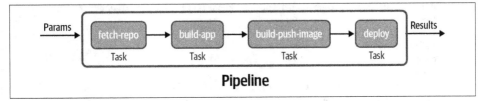

Figure 6-7. Pipeline

In this example you'll see a PersistentVolumeClaim (*https://oreil.ly/Opio5*) as a Workspace because here the data is shared among different Tasks so we need to persist it:

```
apiVersion: v1
kind: PersistentVolumeClaim
metadata:
  name: app-source-pvc
spec:
  accessModes:
    - ReadWriteOnce
  resources:
    requests:
      storage: 1Gi
```

As usual, you can create the resource with `kubectl`:

```
kubectl create -f app-source-pvc.yaml
```

You should see the following output:

```
persistentvolumeclaim/app-source-pvc created

kubectl get pvc

NAME             STATUS    VOLUME                                      CAPACITY
ACCESS MODES     STORAGECLASS    AGE
app-source-pvc   Bound     pvc-e85ade46-aaca-4f3f-b644-d8ff99fd9d5e    1Gi
RWO              standard        61s
```

> In Minikube you have a default StorageClass (*https://oreil.ly/ ZiPnA*) that provides dynamic storage for the cluster. If you are using another Kubernetes cluster, please make sure you have a dynamic storage support.

The Pipeline definition now is:

```
apiVersion: tekton.dev/v1beta1
kind: Pipeline
metadata:
  name: tekton-greeter-pipeline-hub
spec:
  params:
  - default: https://github.com/gitops-cookbook/tekton-tutorial-greeter.git
    name: GIT_REPO
    type: string
  - default: master
    name: GIT_REF
    type: string
  - default: quay.io/gitops-cookbook/tekton-greeter:latest
    name: DESTINATION_IMAGE
    type: string
  - default: kubectl create deploy tekton-greeter --image=quay.io/gitops-cookbook/
tekton-greeter:latest
```

```yaml
    name: SCRIPT
    type: string
- default: ./Dockerfile
  name: CONTEXT_DIR
  type: string
- default: .
  name: IMAGE_DOCKERFILE
  type: string
- default: .
  name: IMAGE_CONTEXT_DIR
  type: string
tasks:
- name: fetch-repo
  params:
  - name: url
    value: $(params.GIT_REPO)
  - name: revision
    value: $(params.GIT_REF)
  - name: deleteExisting
    value: "true"
  - name: verbose
    value: "true"
  taskRef:
    kind: Task
    name: git-clone
  workspaces:
  - name: output
    workspace: app-source
- name: build-app
  params:
  - name: GOALS
    value:
    - -DskipTests
    - clean
    - package
  - name: CONTEXT_DIR
    value: $(params.CONTEXT_DIR)
  runAfter:
  - fetch-repo
  taskRef:
    kind: Task
    name: maven
  workspaces:
  - name: maven-settings
    workspace: maven-settings
  - name: source
    workspace: app-source
- name: build-push-image
  params:
  - name: IMAGE
    value: $(params.DESTINATION_IMAGE)
  - name: DOCKERFILE
    value: $(params.IMAGE_DOCKERFILE)
  - name: CONTEXT
```

```
      value: $(params.IMAGE_CONTEXT_DIR)
    runAfter:
    - build-app
    taskRef:
      kind: Task
      name: buildah
    workspaces:
    - name: source
      workspace: app-source
  - name: deploy
    params:
    - name: script
      value: $(params.SCRIPT)
    runAfter:
    - build-push-image
    taskRef:
      kind: Task
      name: kubernetes-actions
  workspaces:
  - name: app-source
  - name: maven-settings
```

Let's create the resource:

```
kubectl create -f tekton-greeter-pipeline-hub.yaml
```

> We are using the same Secret and ServiceAccount defined in
> Recipe 6.5 to log in against Quay.io in order to push the container
> image.

You can now start the Pipeline as follows:

```
tkn pipeline start tekton-greeter-pipeline-hub \
  --serviceaccount='tekton-deployer-sa' \
  --param GIT_REPO='https://github.com/gitops-cookbook/tekton-tutorial-
greeter.git' \
  --param GIT_REF='master' \
  --param CONTEXT_DIR='quarkus' \
  --param DESTINATION_IMAGE='quay.io/gitops-cookbook/tekton-greeter:latest' \
  --param IMAGE_DOCKERFILE='quarkus/Dockerfile' \
  --param IMAGE_CONTEXT_DIR='quarkus' \
  --param SCRIPT='kubectl create deploy tekton-greeter --image=quay.io/gitops-
cookbook/tekton-greeter:latest' \
  --workspace name=app-source,claimName=app-source-pvc \
  --workspace name=maven-settings,emptyDir="" \
  --use-param-defaults \
  --showlog

[fetch-repo : clone] + CHECKOUT_DIR=/workspace/output/
[fetch-repo : clone] + /ko-app/git-init '-url=https://github.com/gitops-cookbook/
tekton-tutorial-greeter.git' '-revision=master' '-refspec=' '-path=/workspace/out
put/' '-sslVerify=true' '-submodules=true' '-depth=1' '-sparseCheckoutDirectories='
```

```
[fetch-repo : clone] {"level":"info","ts":1660819038.5526028,"caller":"git/
git.go:170","msg":"Successfully cloned https://github.com/gitops-cookbook/tekton-
tutorial-greeter.git @ d9291c456db1ce29177b77ffeaa9b71ad80a50e6 (grafted, HEAD, ori
gin/master) in path /workspace/output/"}
[fetch-repo : clone] {"level":"info","ts":1660819038.5722632,"caller":"git/
git.go:208","msg":"Successfully initialized and updated submodules in path /work
space/output/"}
[fetch-repo : clone] + cd /workspace/output/
[fetch-repo : clone] + git rev-parse HEAD
[fetch-repo : clone] + RESULT_SHA=d9291c456db1ce29177b77ffeaa9b71ad80a50e6
[fetch-repo : clone] + EXIT_CODE=0
[fetch-repo : clone] + '[' 0 '!=' 0 ]
[fetch-repo : clone] + printf '%s' d9291c456db1ce29177b77ffeaa9b71ad80a50e6
[fetch-repo : clone] + printf '%s' https://github.com/gitops-cookbook/tekton-
tutorial-greeter.git
...
[build-app : mvn-goals] [INFO] [org.jboss.threads] JBoss Threads version
3.1.1.Final
[build-app : mvn-goals] [INFO] [io.quarkus.deployment.QuarkusAugmentor] Quarkus
augmentation completed in 1296ms
[build-app : mvn-goals] [INFO]
------------------------------------------------------------------------
[build-app : mvn-goals] [INFO] BUILD SUCCESS
[build-app : mvn-goals] [INFO]
------------------------------------------------------------------------
[build-app : mvn-goals] [INFO] Total time:  03:18 min
[build-app : mvn-goals] [INFO] Finished at: 2022-08-18T10:31:00Z
[build-app : mvn-goals] [INFO]
------------------------------------------------------------------------
[build-push-image : build] STEP 1/2: FROM registry.access.redhat.com/ubi8/
openjdk-11
[build-push-image : build] Trying to pull registry.access.redhat.com/ubi8/
openjdk-11:latest...
[build-push-image : build] Getting image source signatures
[build-push-image : build] Checking if image destination supports signatures
[build-push-image : build] Copying blob
sha256:e441d34134fac91baa79be3e2bb8fb3dba71ba5c1ea012cb5daeb7180a054687
[build-push-image : build] Copying blob
sha256:1e09a5ee0038fbe06a18e7f355188bbabc387467144abcd435f7544fef395aa1
[build-push-image : build] Copying blob
sha256:0d725b91398ed3db11249808d89e688e62e511bbd4a2e875ed8493ce1febdb2c
[build-push-image : build] Copying blob
sha256:e441d34134fac91baa79be3e2bb8fb3dba71ba5c1ea012cb5daeb7180a054687
[build-push-image : build] Copying blob
sha256:1e09a5ee0038fbe06a18e7f355188bbabc387467144abcd435f7544fef395aa1
[build-push-image : build] Copying blob
sha256:0d725b91398ed3db11249808d89e688e62e511bbd4a2e875ed8493ce1febdb2c
[build-push-image : build] Copying config
sha256:0c308464b19eaa9a01c3fdd6b63a043c160d4eea85e461bbbb7d01d168f6d993
[build-push-image : build] Writing manifest to image destination
[build-push-image : build] Storing signatures
[build-push-image : build] STEP 2/2: COPY target/quarkus-app /deployments/
[build-push-image : build] COMMIT quay.io/gitops-cookbook/tekton-greeter:latest
[build-push-image : build] --> c07e36a8e61
```

```
[build-push-image : build] Successfully tagged quay.io/gitops-cookbook/tekton-
greeter:latest
[build-push-image : build]
c07e36a8e6104d2e5c7d79a6cd34cd7b44eb093c39ef6c1487a37d7bd2305b8a
[build-push-image : build] Getting image source signatures
[build-push-image : build] Copying blob
sha256:7853a7797845542e3825d4f305e4784ea7bf492cd4364fc93b9afba3ac0c9553
[build-push-image : build] Copying blob
sha256:8e0e04b5c700a86f4a112f41e7e767a9d7c539fe3391611313bf76edb07eeab1
[build-push-image : build] Copying blob
sha256:647a854c512bad44709221b6b0973e884f29bcb5a380ee32e95bfb0189b620e6
[build-push-image : build] Copying blob
sha256:69c55192bed92cbb669c88eb3c36449b64ac93ae466abfff2a575273ce05a39e
[build-push-image : build] Copying config
sha256:c07e36a8e6104d2e5c7d79a6cd34cd7b44eb093c39ef6c1487a37d7bd2305b8a
[build-push-image : build] Writing manifest to image destination
[build-push-image : build] Storing signatures
[build-push-image : build]
sha256:12dd3deb6305b9e125309b68418d0bb81f805e0fe7ac93942dc94764aee9f492quay.io/
gitops-cookbook/tekton-greeter:latest
[deploy : kubectl] deployment.apps/tekton-greeter created
```

You can use the Tekton Dashboard to create and visualize your
running Tasks and Pipelines as shown in Figure 6-8.

Figure 6-8. Tekton Dashboard TaskRuns

See Also

- Tekton Catalog (*https://oreil.ly/bnUiR*)

6.8 Using Tekton Triggers to Compile and Package an Application Automatically When a Change Occurs on Git

Problem

You want to automate your CI/CD Pipelines when a change on Git occurs.

Solution

Tekton Triggers (*https://oreil.ly/zVcfe*) is the Tekton component that brings automation for Tasks and Pipelines with Tekton. It is an interesting feature for a GitOps strategy for cloud native CI/CD as it supports external events from a large set of sources such as Git events (Git push or pull requests).

Most Git repository servers support the concept of webhooks, calling to an external source via HTTP(S) when a change in the code repository happens. Tekton provides an API endpoint that supports receiving hooks from remote systems in order to trigger builds. By pointing the code repository's hook at the Tekton resources, automated code/build/deploy pipelines can be achieved.

The installation of Tekton Triggers, which we discussed in Recipe 6.1, brings a set of CRDs to manage event handling for Tasks and Pipelines. In this recipe we will use the following, as illustrated also in Figure 6-9:

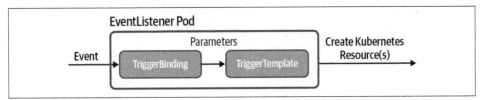

Figure 6-9. Tekton Triggers

TriggerTemplate
: A template for newly created resources. It supports parameters to create specific PipelineRuns.

TriggerBinding
: Validates events and extracts payload fields.

EventListener

Connects `TriggerBindings` and `TriggerTemplates` into an addressable endpoint (the event sink). It uses the extracted event parameters from each `Trigger Binding` (and any supplied static parameters) to create the resources specified in the corresponding `TriggerTemplate`. It also optionally allows an external service to preprocess the event payload via the interceptor field.

Before creating these resources, you need to set up permissions to let Tekton Triggers create Pipelines and Tasks. You can use the setup available from the book's repository (*https://oreil.ly/fPTzU*) with the following command:

```
kubectl apply \
-f https://raw.githubusercontent.com/gitops-cookbook/chapters/main/chapters/ch06/
rbac.yaml
```

This will create a new `ServiceAccount` named `tekton-triggers-sa` that has the permissions needed to interact with the Tekton Pipelines component. As confirmation, from the previous command you should get the following output:

```
serviceaccount/tekton-triggers-sa created
rolebinding.rbac.authorization.k8s.io/triggers-example-eventlistener-binding con-
figured
clusterrolebinding.rbac.authorization.k8s.io/triggers-example-eventlistener-
clusterbinding configured
```

You can now add automation to your Pipelines like the one we defined in Recipe 6.7 creating these three resources:

```
apiVersion: triggers.tekton.dev/v1alpha1
kind: TriggerTemplate
metadata:
  name: tekton-greeter-triggertemplate
spec:
  params:
    - name: git-revision
    - name: git-commit-message
    - name: git-repo-url
    - name: git-repo-name
    - name: content-type
    - name: pusher-name
  resourcetemplates:
    - apiVersion: tekton.dev/v1beta1
      kind: PipelineRun
      metadata:
        labels:
          tekton.dev/pipeline: tekton-greeter-pipeline-hub
        name: tekton-greeter-pipeline-webhook-$(uid)
      spec:
        params:
          - name: GIT_REPO
            value: $(tt.params.git-repo-url)
          - name: GIT_REF
```

```
            value: $(tt.params.git-revision)
          serviceAccountName: tekton-triggers-example-sa
          pipelineRef:
            name: tekton-greeter-pipeline-hub
          workspaces:
          - name: app-source
            persistentVolumeClaim:
              claimName: app-source-pvc
          - name: maven-settings
            emptyDir: {}
apiVersion: triggers.tekton.dev/v1alpha1
kind: TriggerBinding
metadata:
  name: tekton-greeter-triggerbinding
spec:
  params:
  - name: git-repo-url
    value: $(body.repository.clone_url)
  - name: git-revision
    value: $(body.after)
apiVersion: triggers.tekton.dev/v1alpha1
kind: EventListener
metadata:
  name: tekton-greeter-eventlistener
spec:
  serviceAccountName: tekton-triggers-example-sa
  triggers:
  - bindings:
    - ref: tekton-greeter-triggerbinding
    template:
      ref: tekton-greeter-triggertemplate
```

You can create the resources just listed as follows:

```
kubectl create -f tekton-greeter-triggertemplate.yaml
kubectl create -f tekton-greeter-triggerbinding.yaml
kubectl create -f tekton-greeter-eventlistener.yaml
```

You should get the following output:

```
triggertemplate.triggers.tekton.dev/tekton-greeter-triggertemplate created
triggerbinding.triggers.tekton.dev/tekton-greeter-triggerbinding created
eventlistener.triggers.tekton.dev/tekton-greeter-eventlistener created
```

Contextually, a new pod is created representing the EventListener:

```
kubectl get pods
```

You should get output similar to the following:

```
NAME                                               READY  STATUS   RESTARTS AGE
el-tekton-greeter-eventlistener-5db7b9fcf9-6nrgx   1/1    Running  0        10s
```

The EventListener pod listens for events at a specified port, and it is bound to a Kubernetes Service:

```
kubectl get svc
```

You should get output similar to the following:

```
NAME                                 TYPE        CLUSTER-IP      EXTERNAL-IP↳
  PORT(S)              AGE
el-tekton-greeter-eventlistener      ClusterIP   10.100.36.199   <none>     ↳
  8080/TCP,9000/TCP   10s
...
```

If you are running your Git server outside the cluster (e.g., GitHub or GitLab), you need to expose the Service, for example, with an Ingress (*https://oreil.ly/qAUhw*). Afterwards you can configure webhooks on your Git server using the `EventListener` URL associated to your Ingress.

> With Minikube you can add support for Ingresses with this command: `minikube addons enable ingress`. Then you need to map a hostname for the Ingress.

For the purpose of this book we can just simulate the webhook as it would come from the Git server.

First you can map the `EventListener` Service to your local networking with the following command:

```
kubectl port-forward svc/el-tekton-greeter-eventlistener 8080
```

Then you can invoke the Trigger by making an HTTP request to *http://localhost:8080* using `curl`. The HTTP request must be a POST request containing a JSON payload and it should contain the fields referenced via a `TriggerBinding`. In our case we mapped `body.repository.clone_url` and `body.after`.

> Check the documentation of your Git server to get the list of parameters that a webhook can generate. In this example we are using the GitHub Webhooks reference (*https://oreil.ly/4AUlu*).

To test Triggers, run this command:

```
curl -X POST \
  http://localhost:8080 \
  -H 'Content-Type: application/json' \
  -d '{ "after": "d9291c456db1ce29177b77ffeaa9b71ad80a50e6", "repos
itory": { "clone_url" : "https://github.com/gitops-cookbook/tekton-tutorial-
greeter.git" } }'
```

You should get output similar to the following:

```
{"eventListener":"tekton-greeter-eventlistener","namespace":"default","eventListe
nerUID":"c00567eb-d798-4c4a-946d-f1732fdfc313","eventID":"17dd25bb-a1fe-4f84-8422-
c3abc5f10066"}
```

A new Pipeline now is started and you can check it with the following command:

```
tkn pipelinerun ls
```

You should see it in Running status as follows:

```
tekton-greeter-pipeline-3244b67f-31d3-4597-af1c-3c1aa6693719    4 seconds ago
---          Running
```

See Also

- Tekton Triggers examples (*https://oreil.ly/Xr0ne*)
- Getting Started with Tekton Triggers (*https://oreil.ly/gqKyz*)
- Securing webhooks with event listeners (*https://oreil.ly/iIbXc*)

6.9 Update a Kubernetes Resource Using Kustomize and Push the Change to Git

Problem

You want to use Kustomize in your Tekton Pipelines in order to automate Kubernetes manifests updates.

Solution

As we discussed in Chapter 4, Kustomize is a powerful tool to manage Kubernetes manifests. Kustomize can add, remove, or patch configuration options without forking. In Recipe 4.2 you saw how to update a Kubernetes Deployment with a new container image hash using the kustomize CLI.

In this recipe, you'll see how to let Tekton update it using Kustomize. This is very useful for GitOps as it allows an automated update on Git to the manifests describing an application running on Kubernetes, favoring the interconnection with a GitOps tool such as Argo CD in order to sync resources (see Chapter 7).

When adopting the GitOps approach, it's common to have one or more repositories for the Kubernetes manifests and then one or more repositories for the apps as well.

Thus let's introduce a Task that accepts the Kubernetes manifests repository as a parameter and can update the container image reference as seen in Recipe 4.2:

```
apiVersion: tekton.dev/v1beta1
kind: Task
metadata:
```

```yaml
    annotations:
      tekton.dev/pipelines.minVersion: 0.12.1
      tekton.dev/tags: git
    name: git-update-deployment
    labels:
      app.kubernetes.io/version: '0.2'
      operator.tekton.dev/provider-type: community
spec:
  description: >-
    This Task can be used to update image digest in a Git repo using kustomize.
    It requires a secret with credentials for accessing the git repo.
  params:
    - name: GIT_REPOSITORY
      type: string
    - name: GIT_REF
      type: string
    - name: NEW_IMAGE
      type: string
    - name: NEW_DIGEST
      type: string
    - name: KUSTOMIZATION_PATH
      type: string
  results:
    - description: The commit SHA
      name: commit
  steps:
    - image: 'docker.io/alpine/git:v2.26.2'
      name: git-clone
      resources: {}
      script: >
        rm -rf git-update-digest-workdir

        git clone $(params.GIT_REPOSITORY) -b $(params.GIT_REF)
        git-update-digest-workdir
      workingDir: $(workspaces.workspace.path)
    - image: 'quay.io/wpernath/kustomize-ubi:latest'
      name: update-digest
      resources: {}
      script: >
        cd git-update-digest-workdir/$(params.KUSTOMIZATION_PATH)

        kustomize edit set image $(params.NEW_IMAGE)@$(params.NEW_DIGEST)


        echo "#######################"

        echo "### kustomization.yaml ###"

        echo "#######################"

        cat kustomization.yaml
      workingDir: $(workspaces.workspace.path)
    - image: 'docker.io/alpine/git:v2.26.2'
      name: git-commit
```

```
      resources: {}
      script: |
        cd git-update-digest-workdir

        git config user.email "tektonbot@redhat.com"
        git config user.name "My Tekton Bot"

        git status
        git add $(params.KUSTOMIZATION_PATH)/kustomization.yaml
        git commit -m "[ci] Image digest updated"

        git push

        RESULT_SHA="$(git rev-parse HEAD | tr -d '\n')"
        EXIT_CODE="$?"
        if [ "$EXIT_CODE" != 0 ]
        then
          exit $EXIT_CODE
        fi
        # Make sure we don't add a trailing newline to the result!
        echo -n "$RESULT_SHA" > $(results.commit.path)
      workingDir: $(workspaces.workspace.path)
  workspaces:
    - description: The workspace consisting of maven project.
      name: workspace
```

This Task is composed of three steps:

git-clone
> Clones the Kubernetes manifests repository

update-digest
> Runs kustomize to update the Kubernetes Deployment with a container image hash given as a parameter

git-commit
> Updates the Kubernetes manifest repo with the new container image hash

You can create the Task with the following command:

```
kubectl create -f git-update-deployment-task.yaml
```

You should get the following output:

```
task.tekton.dev/git-update-deployment created
```

You can now add this Task to a Pipeline similar to the one you saw in Recipe 6.7 in order to automate the update of your manifests with Kustomize:

```
apiVersion: tekton.dev/v1beta1
kind: Pipeline
metadata:
  name: pacman-pipeline
spec:
```

```yaml
  params:
  - default: https://github.com/gitops-cookbook/pacman-kikd.git
    name: GIT_REPO
    type: string
  - default: master
    name: GIT_REVISION
    type: string
  - default: quay.io/gitops-cookbook/pacman-kikd
    name: DESTINATION_IMAGE
    type: string
  - default: .
    name: CONTEXT_DIR
    type: string
  - default: 'https://github.com/gitops-cookbook/pacman-kikd-manifests.git'
    name: CONFIG_GIT_REPO
    type: string
  - default: main
    name: CONFIG_GIT_REVISION
    type: string
  tasks:
  - name: fetch-repo
    params:
    - name: url
      value: $(params.GIT_REPO)
    - name: revision
      value: $(params.GIT_REVISION)
    - name: deleteExisting
      value: "true"
    taskRef:
      name: git-clone
    workspaces:
    - name: output
      workspace: app-source
  - name: build-app
    taskRef:
      name: maven
    params:
      - name: GOALS
        value:
          - -DskipTests
          - clean
          - package
      - name: CONTEXT_DIR
        value: "$(params.CONTEXT_DIR)"
    workspaces:
      - name: maven-settings
        workspace: maven-settings
      - name: source
        workspace: app-source
    runAfter:
      - fetch-repo
  - name: build-push-image
    taskRef:
      name: buildah
```

```
    params:
    - name: IMAGE
      value: "$(params.DESTINATION_IMAGE)"
    workspaces:
      - name: source
        workspace: app-source
    runAfter:
      - build-app
- name: git-update-deployment
  params:
  - name: GIT_REPOSITORY
    value: $(params.CONFIG_GIT_REPO)
  - name: NEW_IMAGE
    value: $(params.DESTINATION_IMAGE)
  - name: NEW_DIGEST
    value: $(tasks.build-push-image.results.IMAGE_DIGEST) ❶
  - name: KUSTOMIZATION_PATH
    value: env/dev
  - name: GIT_REF
    value: $(params.CONFIG_GIT_REVISION)
  runAfter:
    - build-push-image
  taskRef:
    kind: Task
    name: git-update-deployment
  workspaces:
  - name: workspace
    workspace: app-source
workspaces:
  - name: app-source
  - name: maven-settings
```

❶ As you can see from this example, you can take a result of a previous Task as an input for the following one. In this case the hash of the container image generated by the `build-push-image` Task is used to update the manifests with Kustomize.

You can create the Pipeline with the following command:

```
kubectl create -f pacman-pipeline.yaml
```

You should get the following output:

```
pipeline.tekton.dev/pacman-pipeline created
```

The `git-commit` step requires authentication to your Git server in order to push the updates to the repo. Since this example is on GitHub, we are using a GitHub Personal Access Token (see Recipe 6.4) attached to the ServiceAccount `tekton-bot-sa`.

Make sure to add the repo and registry's Kubernetes Secrets as described in Recipes 6.4 and 6.5:

```
kubectl patch serviceaccount tekton-bot-sa -p '{"secrets": [{"name": "git-
secret"}]}'
kubectl patch serviceaccount tekton-bot-sa \
 -p '{"secrets": [{"name": "containerregistry-
secret"}]}'
```

 Make sure you have created a PVC for the Pipeline as defined in Recipe 6.7.

Now you can start the Pipeline as follows:

```
tkn pipeline start pacman-pipeline \
  --serviceaccount='tekton-bot-sa' \
  --param GIT_REPO='https://github.com/gitops-cookbook/pacman-kikd.git' \
  --param GIT_REVISION='main' \
  --param DESTINATION_IMAGE='quay.io/gitops-cookbook/pacman-kikd:latest' \
  --param CONFIG_GIT_REPO='https://github.com/gitops-cookbook/pacman-kikd-
manifests.git' \
  --param CONFIG_GIT_REVISION='main' \
  --workspace name=app-source,claimName=app-source-pvc \
  --workspace name=maven-settings,emptyDir="" \
  --use-param-defaults \
  --showlog
```

6.10 Update a Kubernetes Resource Using Helm and Create a Pull Request

Problem

You want to automate the deployment of Helm-packaged apps with a Tekton Pipeline.

Solution

In Chapter 5 we discussed Helm and how it can be used to manage applications on Kubernetes in a convenient way. In this recipe you'll see how to automate Helm-powered deployments through a Pipeline in order to install or update an application running on Kubernetes.

As shown in Recipe 6.7, you can use Tekton Hub to find and install Tekton Tasks. In fact, you can use the helm-upgrade-from-repo (*https://oreil.ly/oR6GU*) Task to have Helm support for your Pipelines.

To install it, run this command:

```
tkn hub install task helm-upgrade-from-repo
```

This Task can install a Helm Chart from a Helm repository. For this example, we provide a Helm repository in this book's repository (*https://oreil.ly/lroxo*) that you can add with the following command:

```
helm repo add gitops-cookbook https://gitops-cookbook.github.io/helm-charts/
```

You should get the following output:

```
"gitops-cookbook" has been added to your repositories
```

You can install the Helm Chart with the following command:

```
helm install pacman gitops-cookbook/pacman
```

You should get output similar to the following:

```
NAME: pacman
LAST DEPLOYED: Mon Aug 15 17:02:21 2022
NAMESPACE: default
STATUS: deployed
REVISION: 1
TEST SUITE: None
USER-SUPPLIED VALUES:
{}
```

The app should be now deployed and running on Kubernetes:

```
kubectl get pods -l=app.kubernetes.io/name=pacman
```

You should get the following output:

```
NAME                      READY   STATUS    RESTARTS   AGE
pacman-6798d65d84-9mt8p   1/1     Running   0          30s
```

Now let's update the Deployment with a Tekton Task running a `helm upgrade` with the following TaskRun:

```
apiVersion: tekton.dev/v1beta1
kind: TaskRun
metadata:
  generateName: helm-pacman-run-
spec:
  serviceAccountName: tekton-deployer-sa   ❶
  taskRef:
    name: helm-upgrade-from-repo
  params:
  - name: helm_repo
    value: https://gitops-cookbook.github.io/helm-charts/
  - name: chart_name
    value: gitops-cookbook/pacman
  - name: release_version
    value: 0.1.0
  - name: release_name
```

```
    value: pacman
  - name: overwrite_values
    value: replicaCount=2 
```
 ❷

 ❶   The `helm-upgrade-from-repo` Task needs permission to list objects in the work-ing namespace, so you need a `ServiceAccount` with special permissions as seen in Recipe 6.6.

❷   You can override values in the Chart's *values.yaml* file by adding them in this param. Here we are setting up two replicas for the Pac-Man game.

Run the Task with the following command:

```
kubectl create -f helm-pacman-taskrun.yaml
```

You should get output similar to the following:

```
taskrun.tekton.dev/helm-pacman-run-qghx8 created
```

Check logs with `tkn` CLI and select the running Task:

```
tkn taskrun logs -f
```

You should get output similar to the following, where you can see the Helm upgrade has been successfully performed:

```
[upgrade-from-repo] current installed helm releases
[upgrade-from-repo] NAME          NAMESPACE       REVISION        UPDA-
TED                                STATUS          CHART           APP
VERSION
[upgrade-from-repo] pacman        default         1               2022-08-15
17:02:21.633934129 +0200 +0200    deployed        pacman-0.1.0    1.0.0
[upgrade-from-repo] parsing helms repo name...
[upgrade-from-repo] adding helm repo...
[upgrade-from-repo] "gitops-cookbook" has been added to your repositories
[upgrade-from-repo] adding updating repo...
[upgrade-from-repo] Hang tight while we grab the latest from your chart reposito-
ries...
[upgrade-from-repo] ...Successfully got an update from the "gitops-cookbook" chart
repository
[upgrade-from-repo] Update Complete. ❀Happy Helming!❀
[upgrade-from-repo] installing helm chart...
[upgrade-from-repo] history.go:56: [debug] getting history for release pacman
[upgrade-from-repo] upgrade.go:123: [debug] preparing upgrade for pacman
[upgrade-from-repo] upgrade.go:131: [debug] performing update for pacman
[upgrade-from-repo] upgrade.go:303: [debug] creating upgraded release for pacman
[upgrade-from-repo] client.go:203: [debug] checking 2 resources for changes
[upgrade-from-repo] client.go:466: [debug] Looks like there are no changes for
Service "pacman"
[upgrade-from-repo] wait.go:47: [debug] beginning wait for 2 resources with time-
out of 5m0s
[upgrade-from-repo] ready.go:277: [debug] Deployment is not ready: default/pacman.
1 out of 2 expected pods are ready
[upgrade-from-repo] ready.go:277: [debug] Deployment is not ready: default/pacman.
```

```
1 out of 2 expected pods are ready
[upgrade-from-repo] ready.go:277: [debug] Deployment is not ready: default/pacman.
1 out of 2 expected pods are ready
[upgrade-from-repo] upgrade.go:138: [debug] updating status for upgraded release
for pacman
[upgrade-from-repo] Release "pacman" has been upgraded. Happy Helming!
[upgrade-from-repo] NAME: pacman
[upgrade-from-repo] LAST DEPLOYED: Mon Aug 15 15:23:31 2022
[upgrade-from-repo] NAMESPACE: default
[upgrade-from-repo] STATUS: deployed
[upgrade-from-repo] REVISION: 2
[upgrade-from-repo] TEST SUITE: None
[upgrade-from-repo] USER-SUPPLIED VALUES:
[upgrade-from-repo] replicaCount: 2
[upgrade-from-repo]
[upgrade-from-repo] COMPUTED VALUES:
[upgrade-from-repo] image:
[upgrade-from-repo]   containerPort: 8080
[upgrade-from-repo]   pullPolicy: Always
[upgrade-from-repo]   repository: quay.io/gitops-cookbook/pacman-kikd
[upgrade-from-repo]   tag: 1.0.0
[upgrade-from-repo] replicaCount: 2
[upgrade-from-repo] securityContext: {}
[upgrade-from-repo]
[upgrade-from-repo] HOOKS:
[upgrade-from-repo] MANIFEST:
[upgrade-from-repo] ---
[upgrade-from-repo] # Source: pacman/templates/service.yaml
[upgrade-from-repo] apiVersion: v1
[upgrade-from-repo] kind: Service
[upgrade-from-repo] metadata:
[upgrade-from-repo]   labels:
[upgrade-from-repo]     app.kubernetes.io/name: pacman
[upgrade-from-repo]   name: pacman
[upgrade-from-repo] spec:
[upgrade-from-repo]   ports:
[upgrade-from-repo]   - name: http
[upgrade-from-repo]     port: 8080
[upgrade-from-repo]     targetPort: 8080
[upgrade-from-repo]   selector:
[upgrade-from-repo]     app.kubernetes.io/name: pacman
[upgrade-from-repo] ---
[upgrade-from-repo] # Source: pacman/templates/deployment.yaml
[upgrade-from-repo] apiVersion: apps/v1
[upgrade-from-repo] kind: Deployment
[upgrade-from-repo] metadata:
[upgrade-from-repo]   name: pacman
[upgrade-from-repo]   labels:
[upgrade-from-repo]     app.kubernetes.io/name: pacman
[upgrade-from-repo]     app.kubernetes.io/version: "1.0.0"
[upgrade-from-repo] spec:
[upgrade-from-repo]   replicas: 2
[upgrade-from-repo]   selector:
[upgrade-from-repo]     matchLabels:
```

```
[upgrade-from-repo]      app.kubernetes.io/name: pacman
[upgrade-from-repo]   template:
[upgrade-from-repo]     metadata:
[upgrade-from-repo]       labels:
[upgrade-from-repo]         app.kubernetes.io/name: pacman
[upgrade-from-repo]     spec:
[upgrade-from-repo]       containers:
[upgrade-from-repo]         - image: "quay.io/gitops-cookbook/pacman-kikd:1.0.0"
[upgrade-from-repo]           imagePullPolicy: Always
[upgrade-from-repo]           securityContext:
[upgrade-from-repo]             {}
[upgrade-from-repo]           name: pacman
[upgrade-from-repo]           ports:
[upgrade-from-repo]             - containerPort: 8080
[upgrade-from-repo]               name: http
[upgrade-from-repo]               protocol: TCP
[upgrade-from-repo]

kubectl get deploy -l=app.kubernetes.io/name=pacman

pacman              2/2     2         2          9s
```

6.11 Use Drone to Create a Pipeline for Kubernetes

Problem

You want to create a CI/CD pipeline for Kubernetes with Drone.

Solution

Drone (*https://www.drone.io*) is an open source project for cloud native continuous integration (CI). It uses YAML build files to define and execute build pipelines inside containers.

It has two main components:

Server
    Integrates with popular SCMs such as GitHub, GitLab, or Gitea

Runner
    Acts as an agent running on a certain platform

You can install the Server of your choice following the documentation (*https://oreil.ly/ K1ZR2*) and install the Kubernetes Runner (*https://oreil.ly/3vydl*).

In this example you will create a Java Maven-based pipeline using the Pac-Man app. First, install the Drone CLI for your OS; you can get it from the official website here (*https://oreil.ly/cdI9Y*).

On macOS, drone is available through Homebrew (*https://brew.sh*) as follows:

```
brew tap drone/drone && brew install drone
```

Then configure Drone, copy the `DRONE_TOKEN` from your instance under the Drone Account settings page, then create/update the file called *.envrc.local* and add the variables to override:

```
export DRONE_TOKEN="<YOUR-TOKEN>"
```

Ensure the token is loaded:

```
drone info
```

Now activate the repo in Drone:

```
drone repo enable https://github.com/gitops-cookbook/pacman-kikd.git
```

Similarly to Tekton, Drone's pipeline will compile, test, and build the app. Then it will create and push the container image to a registry.

Add credentials to your container registry as follows (here, we're using Quay.io):

```
drone secret add --name image_registry \
--data quay.io https://github.com/gitops-cookbook/pacman-kikd.git

drone secret add --name image_registry_user \
--data YOUR_REGISTRY_USER https://github.com/gitops-cookbook/pacman-kikd.git

drone secret add --name image_registry_password \
--data YOUR_REGISTRY_PASS https://github.com/gitops-cookbook/pacman-kikd.git

drone secret add --name destination_image \
--data quay.io/YOUR_REGISTRY_USER>/pacman-kikd.git https://github.com/gitops-
cookbook/pacman-kikd.git
```

Create a file called *.drone.yaml* as follows:

```
kind: pipeline
type: docker
name: java-pipeline
platform:
  os: linux
  arch: arm64
trigger:
  branch:
    - main
clone:
  disable: true
steps:
  - name: clone sources
    image: alpine/git
    pull: if-not-exists
```

```
    commands:
      - git clone https://github.com/gitops-cookbook/pacman-kikd.git .
      - git checkout $DRONE_COMMIT
  - name: maven-build
    image: maven:3-jdk-11
    commands:
      - mvn install -DskipTests=true -B
      - mvn test -B
  - name: publish
    image: plugins/docker:20.13
    pull: if-not-exists
    settings:
      tags: "latest"
      dockerfile: Dockerfile
      insecure: true
      mtu: 1400
      username:
        from_secret: image_registry_user
      password:
        from_secret: image_registry_password
      registry:
        from_secret: image_registry
      repo:
        from_secret: destination_image
```

Start the pipeline:

```
drone exec --pipeline=java-pipeline
```

 You can also trigger the pipeline to start by pushing to your Git repo.

See Also

- Example Maven Pipeline from Drone docs (*https://oreil.ly/YzWcx*)
- Complete Quarkus pipeline example in Drone (*https://oreil.ly/eVT1T*)

6.12 Use GitHub Actions for CI

Problem

You want to use GitHub Actions for CI in order to compile and package an app as a container image ready to be deployed in CD.

Solution

GitHub Actions (*https://oreil.ly/hCOUp*) are event-driven automation tasks available for any GitHub repository. An event automatically triggers the workflow, which contains a job. The job then uses steps to control the order in which actions are run. These actions are the commands that automate software building, testing, and deployment.

In this recipe, you will add a GitHub Action for building the Pac-Man game container image, and pushing it to the GitHub Container Registry (*https://oreil.ly/Bzq7l*).

 As GitHub Actions are connected to repositories, you can fork the Pac-Man repository from this book's code repositories to add your GitHub Actions. See the documentation about forking repositories (*https://oreil.ly/O6HtM*) for more info on this topic.

GitHub Actions workflows run into environments (*https://oreil.ly/uXOQ7*) and they can reference an environment to use the environment's protection rules and secrets.

Workflows and jobs are defined with a YAML file containing all the needed steps. Inside your repository, you can create one with the path `.github/workflows/pacman-ci-action.yml`:

```
# This is a basic workflow to help you get started with Actions

name: pacman-ci-action ❶

env: ❷
  IMAGE_REGISTRY: ghcr.io/${{ github.repository_owner }}
  REGISTRY_USER: ${{ github.actor }}
  REGISTRY_PASSWORD: ${{ github.token }}
  APP_NAME: pacman
  IMAGE_TAGS: 1.0.0 ${{ github.sha }}

# Controls when the workflow will run
on:
  # Triggers the workflow on push or pull request events but only for the
  # "main" branch
  push: ❸
    branches: [ "main" ]
  pull_request:
    branches: [ "main" ]

  # Allows you to run this workflow manually from the Actions tab
  workflow_dispatch:

# A workflow run is made up of one or more jobs that can run sequentially or in
# parallel
jobs:
```

```
# This workflow contains a single job called "build-and-push"
build-and-push: ❹
  # The type of runner that the job will run on
  runs-on: ubuntu-latest

  # Steps represent a sequence of tasks that will be executed as part of the
  # job
  steps: ❺
    # Checks-out your repository under $GITHUB_WORKSPACE, so your job can
    # access it
    - uses: actions/checkout@v3

    - name: Set up JDK 11
      uses: actions/setup-java@v3
      with:
        java-version: '11'
        distribution: 'adopt'
        cache: maven

    - name: Build with Maven
      run: mvn --batch-mode package

    - name: Buildah Action ❻
      id: build-image
      uses: redhat-actions/buildah-build@v2
      with:
        image: ${{ env.IMAGE_REGISTRY }}/${{ env.APP_NAME }}
        tags: ${{ env.IMAGE_TAGS }}
        containerfiles: |
          ./Dockerfile
    - name: Push to Registry ❼
      id: push-to-registry
      uses: redhat-actions/push-to-registry@v2
      with:
        image: ${{ steps.build-image.outputs.image }}
        tags: ${{ steps.build-image.outputs.tags }}
        registry: ${{ env.IMAGE_REGISTRY }}
        username: ${{ env.REGISTRY_USER }}
        password: ${{ env.REGISTRY_PASSWORD }}
```

❶ Name of the Action.

❷ Environment variables to be used in the workflow. This includes default envi-ronment variables (*https://oreil.ly/qNE6p*) and the Secret you added to the environment.

❸ Here's where you define which type of trigger you want for this workflow. In this case, any change to the repository (Push) to the master branch will trigger the action to start. Check out the documentation for a full list of triggers (*https://oreil.ly/lGgAE*) that can be used.

❹ Name of this Job.

❺ List of steps; each step contains an action for the pipeline.

❻ Buildah Build (*https://oreil.ly/IcyGC*). This action builds container images using Buildah.

❼ Push to Registry (*https://oreil.ly/HcSUl*). This action is used to push to the GitHub Registry using built-in credentials available for GitHub repository owners.

After each Git push or pull request, a new run of the action is performed as shown in Figure 6-10.

 GitHub offers its own container registry available at ghcr.io, and container images are referenced as part of the GitHub Packages (*https://oreil.ly/aPNi5*). By default the images are public. See this book's repository (*https://oreil.ly/EG1zx*) as a reference.

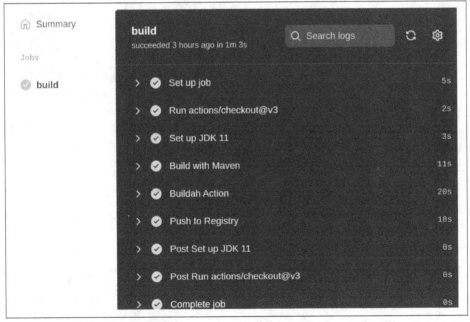

Figure 6-10. GitHub Actions Jobs

See Also

- GitHub Actions Jobs (*https://oreil.ly/44Qt8*)
- Red Hat Actions (*https://oreil.ly/hFcCd*)
- Deploy to Kubernetes cluster Action (*https://oreil.ly/7PaeU*)

CHAPTER 7

Argo CD

In the previous chapter, you learned about Tekton and other engines such as GitHub Actions to implement the continuous integration (CI) part of a project.

Although CI is important because it's where you build the application and check that nothing has been broken (running unit tests, component tests, etc.), there is still a missing part: how to deploy this application to an environment (a Kubernetes cluster) using the GitOps methodology and not creating a script running `kubectl`/ `helm` commands.

As Daniel Bryant puts it, "If you weren't using SSH in the past to deploy your application in production, don't use `kubectl` to do it in Kubernetes."

In this chapter, we'll introduce you to Argo CD, a declarative, GitOps continuous delivery (CD) tool for Kubernetes. In the first part of the section, we'll see the deployment of an application using Argo CD (Recipes 7.1 and 7.2).

Argo CD not only supports the deployment of plain Kubernetes manifests, but also the deployment of Kustomize projects (Recipe 7.3) and Helm projects (Recipe 7.4).

A typical operation done in Kubernetes is a rolling update to a new version of the container, and Argo CD integrates with another tool to make this process smooth (Recipe 7.5).

Delivering complex applications might require some orchestration on when and how the application must be deployed and released (Recipes 7.7 and 7.8).

We'll see how to:

- Install and deploy the first application.
- Use automatic deployment and self-healing applications.

- Execute a rolling update when a new container is released.

- Give an order on the execution.

In this chapter, we are using the `https://github.com/gitops-cookbook/gitops-cookbook-sc.git` GitHub repository as source directory. To run it successfully in this chapter, you should fork it and use it in the YAML files provided in the examples.

7.1 Deploy an Application Using Argo CD

Problem

You want Argo CD to deploy an application defined in a Git repository.

Solution

Create an `Application` resource to set up Argo CD to deploy the application.

To install Argo CD, create the `argocd` namespace and apply the Argo CD installation manifest:

```
kubectl apply -n argocd \
 -f https://raw.githubusercontent.com/argoproj/argo-cd/v2.3.4/manifests/install.yaml
```

Optional Steps

It's not mandatory to install the Argo CD CLI tool, or expose the Argo CD server service to access the Argo CD Dashboard. Still, in this book, we'll use them in the recipes to show you the final result after applying the manifests. So, although not mandatory, we encourage you to follow the next steps to be aligned with the book.

To install the `argocd` CLI tool, go to the Argo CD CLI GitHub release page (*https://oreil.ly/kU9LS*) and in the Assets section, download the tool for your platform.

After installing the `argocd` tool, the `argocd-server` Kubernetes Service needs to be exposed. You can use any technique such as Ingress or set the service as `LoadBalancer` but we'll use the `kubectl port-forwarding` to connect to the API server without exposing the service:

```
kubectl port-forward svc/argocd-server -n argocd 9090:443
```

At this point, you can access the Argo CD server using *http://localhost:9090*.

The initial password for the `admin` account is generated automatically in a secret named `argocd-initial-admin-secret` in the `argocd` namespace:

```
argoPass=$(kubectl -n argocd get secret argocd-initial-admin-secret -o json
path="{.data.password}" | base64 -d)
```

```
argoURL=localhost:9090

argocd login --insecure --grpc-web $argoURL  --username admin --password $argo
Pass

'admin:login' logged in successfully
```
You should use the same credentials to access the Argo CD UI.

Let's make Argo CD deploy a simple web application showing a box with a configured color. The application is composed of three Kubernetes manifest files, including
a Namespace, a Deployment, and a Service definition.

The files are located in the ch07/bgd (*https://oreil.ly/DAH50*) folder of the book's
repository.

All these files are known as an Application in Argo CD. Therefore, you must define
it as such to apply these manifests in your cluster.

Let's check the Argo CD Application resource file used for deploying the
application:

```
apiVersion: argoproj.io/v1alpha1
kind: Application
metadata:
  name: bgd-app
  namespace: argocd ❶
spec:
  destination: ❷
    namespace: bgd
    server: https://kubernetes.default.svc
  project: default ❸
  source:
    repoURL: https://github.com/gitops-cookbook/gitops-cookbook-sc.git ❹
    path: ch07/bgd ❺
    targetRevision: main ❻
```

❶ Namespace where Argo CD is installed

❷ Target cluster and namespace

❸ Installing the application in Argo CD's default project

❹ The manifest repo where the YAML resides

❺ The path to look for manifests

❻ Branch to checkout

In the terminal window, run the following command to register the Argo CD application:

```
kubectl apply -f manual-bgd-app.yaml
```

At this point, the application is registered as an Argo CD application.

You can check the status using either `argocd` or the UI; run the following command to list applications using the CLI too:

```
argocd app list
```

And the output is something like:

```
NAME      CLUSTER                          NAMESPACE  PROJECT  STATUS
bgd-app   https://kubernetes.default.svc   bgd        default  OutOfSync
```

The important field here is `STATUS`. It's `OutOfSync`, which means the application is registered, and there is a drift between the current status (in this case, no application deployed) and the content in the Git repository (the application deployment files).

You'll notice that no pods are running if you get all the pods from the `bgd` namespace:

```
kubectl get pods -n bgd

No resources found in bgd namespace.
```

Argo CD doesn't synchronize the application automatically by default. It just shows a divergence, and the user is free to fix it by triggering a synchronized operation.

With the CLI, you synchronize the application by running the following command in a terminal:

```
argocd app sync bgd-app
```

And the ouput of the command shows all the important information regarding the deployment:

```
Name:            bgd-app
Project:         default
Server:          https://kubernetes.default.svc
Namespace:       bgd
URL:             https://openshift-gitops-server-openshift-gitops.apps.open-
shift.sotogcp.com/applications/bgd-app
Repo:            https://github.com/lordofthejars/gitops-cookbook-sc.git
Target:          main
Path:            ch07/bgd
SyncWindow:      Sync Allowed
Sync Policy:     <none>
Sync Status:     Synced to main (384cd3d)
Health Status:   Progressing

Operation:       Sync
Sync Revision:   384cd3d21c534e75cb6b1a6921a6768925b81244
Phase:           Succeeded
```

```
Start:              2022-06-16 14:45:12 +0200 CEST
Finished:           2022-06-16 14:45:13 +0200 CEST
Duration:           1s
Message:            successfully synced (all tasks run)

GROUP   KIND        NAMESPACE   NAME  STATUS   HEALTH        HOOK   MESSAGE
        Namespace   bgd         bgd   Running  Synced               namespace/bgd cre-
ated
        Service     bgd         bgd   Synced   Healthy              service/bgd created
apps    Deployment  bgd         bgd   Synced   Progressing          deploy-
ment.apps/bgd created
        Namespace               bgd   Synced
```

You can synchronize the application from the UI as well, by clicking the SYNC button as shown in Figure 7-1.

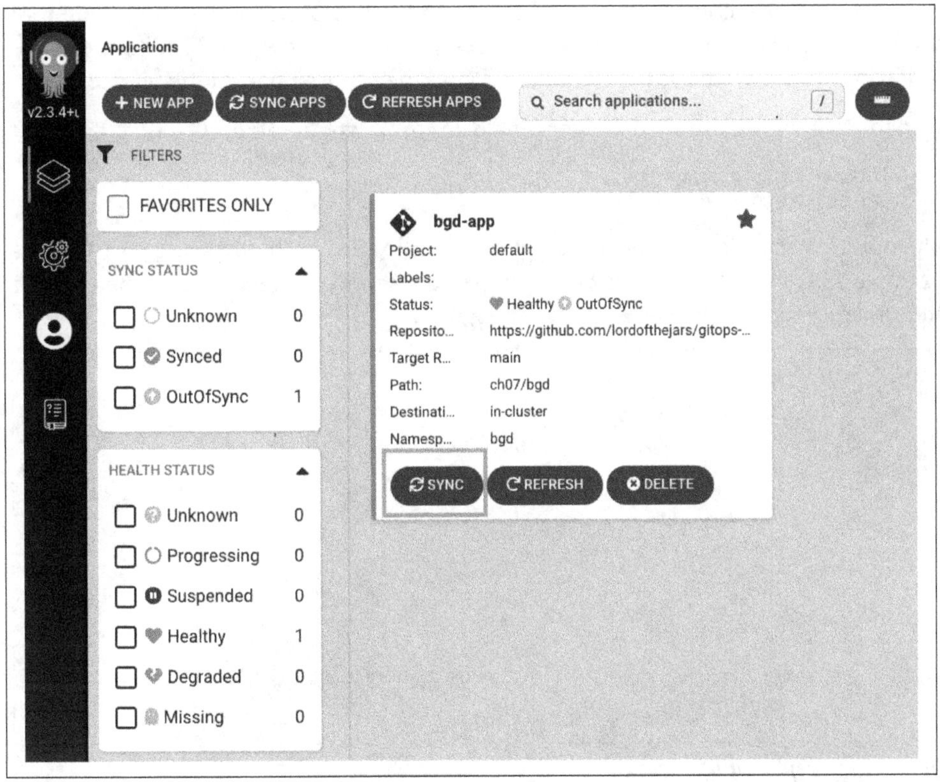

Figure 7-1. Argo CD web console

If you get all the pods from the bgd namespace, you'll notice one pod running:

```
kubectl get pods -n bgd
```

```
NAME                    READY   STATUS    RESTARTS   AGE
bgd-788cb756f7-jll9n    1/1     Running   0          60s
```

And the same for the Service:

```
kubectl get services -n bgd
```

```
NAME   TYPE        CLUSTER-IP      EXTERNAL-IP   PORT(S)
bgd    ClusterIP   172.30.35.199   <none>        8080:32761/TCP ❶
```

❶ Exposed port is 32761

In the following sections, you'll need to access the deployed service to validate that it's deployed. There are several ways to access services deployed to Minikube; for the following chapters, we use the Minikube IP and the exposed port of the service.

Run the following command in a terminal window to get the Minikube IP:

```
minikube ip -p gitops
192.168.59.100
```

Open a browser window, set the previous IP followed by the exposed port (in this example 192.168.59.100:32761), and access the service to validate that the color of the circles in the box is blue, as shown in Figure 7-2.

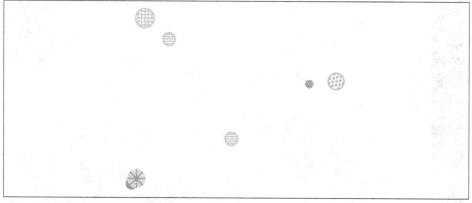

Figure 7-2. Deployed application

Discussion

Now it's time to update the application deployment files. This time we will change the value of an environment variable defined in the *bgd-deployment.yaml* file.

Open *ch07/bgd/bgd-deployment.yaml* in your file editor and change the COLOR environment variable value from blue to green:

```
spec:
  containers:
  - image: quay.io/redhatworkshops/bgd:latest
    name: bgd
    env:
    - name: COLOR
      value: "green"
```

In a terminal run the following commands to commit and push the file so the change is available for Argo CD:

```
git add .
git commit -m "Updates color"

git push origin main
```

With the change pushed, check the status of the application again:

```
argocd app list

NAME     CLUSTER                        NAMESPACE PROJECT STATUS
bgd-app  https://kubernetes.default.svc bgd       default Sync
```

We see the application status is Sync. This happens because Argo CD uses a polling approach to detect divergences between what's deployed and what's defined in Git. After some time (by default, it's 3 minutes), the application status will be OutOfSync:

```
argocd app list
NAME     CLUSTER                        NAMESPACE PROJECT STATUS    HEALTH
bgd-app  https://kubernetes.default.svc bgd       default OutOfSync Healthy
```

To synchronize the changes, run the sync subcommand:

```
argocd app sync bgd-app
```

After some seconds, access the service and validate that the circles are green, as shown in Figure 7-3.

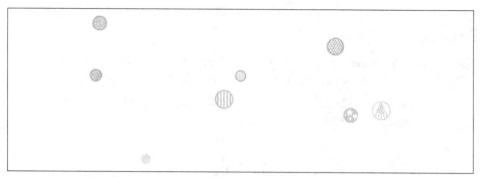

Figure 7-3. Deployed application

To remove the application, use the CLI tool or the UI:

```
argocd app delete bgd-app
```

Also, revert the changes done in the Git repository to get the initial version of the application and push them:

```
git revert HEAD
```

```
git push origin main
```

7.2 Automatic Synchronization

Problem

You want Argo CD to automatically update resources when there are changes.

Solution

Use the `syncPolicy` section with an `automated` policy.

Argo CD can automatically synchronize an application when it detects differences between the manifests in Git and the Kubernetes cluster.

A benefit of automatic sync is that there is no need to log in to the Argo CD API, with the security implications that involves (managing secrets, network, etc.), and the use of the `argocd` tool. Instead, when a manifest is changed and pushed to the Git repository with the changes to the tracking Git repo, the manifests are automatically applied.

Let's modify the previous Argo CD manifest file (`Application`), adding the `sync Policy` section, so changes are deployed automatically:

```
apiVersion: argoproj.io/v1alpha1
kind: Application
metadata:
```

```
  name: bgd-app
  namespace: argocd
spec:
  destination:
    namespace: bgd
    server: https://kubernetes.default.svc
  project: default
  source:
    path: ch07/bgd
    repoURL: https://github.com/gitops-cookbook/gitops-cookbook-sc.git
    targetRevision: main
  syncPolicy: ❶
    automated: {} ❷
```

❶ Starts the synchronization policy configuration section

❷ Argo CD automatically syncs the repo

At this point, we can apply the `Application` file into a running cluster by running the following command:

```
kubectl apply -f bgd/bgd-app.yaml
```

Now, Argo CD deploys the application without executing any other command.

Run the `kubectl` command or check in the Argo CD UI to validate that the deployment is happening:

```
kubectl get pods -n bgd
```

```
NAME                    READY   STATUS    RESTARTS   AGE
bgd-788cb756f7-jll9n    1/1     Running   0          60s
```

Access the service and validate that the circles are blue, as shown in Figure 7-4.

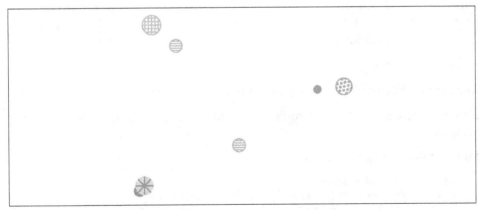

Figure 7-4. Deployed application

To remove the application, use the CLI tool or the UI:

```
argocd app delete bgd-app
```

Discussion

Although Argo CD deploys applications automatically, it uses some default conservative strategies for safety reasons.

Two of these are the pruning of deleted resources and the self-healing of the application in case a change was made in the Kubernetes cluster directly instead of through Git.

By default, Argo CD will not delete (prune) any resource when it detects that it is no longer available in Git, and it will be in an OutOfSync status. If you want Argo CD to delete these resources, you can do it in two ways.

The first way is by manually invoking a sync with the -prune option:

```
argocd app sync --prune
```

The second way is letting Argo CD delete pruned resources automatically by setting the prune attribute to true in the automated section:

```
syncPolicy:
  automated:
    prune: true ❶
```

❶ Enables automatic pruning

Another important concept affecting how the application is automatically updated is self-healing.

Argo CD is configured not to correct any drift made manually in the cluster. For example, Argo CD will let the execution of a kubectl patch directly in the cluster change any configuration parameter of the application.

Let's see it in action.

The color of the circle is set as an environment variable (COLOR).

Now, let's change the COLOR environment variable to green using the kubectl patch command.

Run the following command in the terminal:

```
kubectl -n bgd patch deploy/bgd \
--type='json' -p='[{"op": "replace", "path": "/
spec/template/spec/containers/0/env/0/value", "value":"green"}]'
```

Wait for the rollout to happen:

```
kubectl rollout status deploy/bgd -n bgd
```

If you refresh the browser, you should see green circles now, as shown in Figure 7-5.

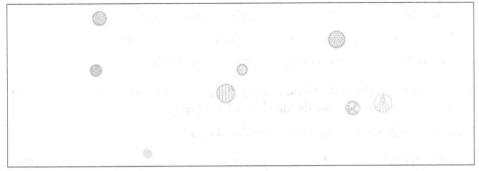

Figure 7-5. Deployed application

Looking over the Argo CD sync status, you'll see that it's OutOfSync as the application and the definition in the Git repository (COLOR: blue) diverges.

Argo CD will not roll back to correct this drift as the selfHeal property default is set to false.

Let's remove the application and deploy a new one, but set selfHeal to true in this case:

```
argocd app delete bgd-app
```

Let's enable the selfHealing property, and repeat the experiment:

```
apiVersion: argoproj.io/v1alpha1
kind: Application
metadata:
  name: bgd-app
  namespace: argocd
spec:
  destination:
    namespace: bgd
    server: https://kubernetes.default.svc
  project: default
  source:
    path: ch07/bgd
    repoURL: https://github.com/gitops-cookbook/gitops-cookbook-sc.git
    targetRevision: main
  syncPolicy:
    automated:
      prune: true
      selfHeal: true    ❶
```

❶ selfHeal set to true to correct any drift

And in the terminal apply the resource:

```
kubectl apply -f bgd/heal-bgd-app.yaml
```

Repeat the previous steps:

1. Open the browser to check that the circles are blue.
2. Reexecute the `kubectl -n bgd patch deploy/bgd ...` command.
3. Refresh the browser and check that the circles are still blue.

Argo CD corrects the drift introduced by the `patch` command, synchronizing the application to the correct state defined in the Git repository.

To remove the application, use the CLI tool or the UI:

```
argocd app delete bgd-app
```

See Also

- Argo CD Automated Sync Policy (*https://oreil.ly/mw4b2*)
- Argo CD Sync Options (*https://oreil.ly/wIleG*)

7.3 Kustomize Integration

Problem

You want to use Argo CD to deploy Kustomize manifests.

Solution

Argo CD supports several different ways in which Kubernetes manifests can be defined:

- Kustomize
- Helm
- Ksonnet
- Jsonnet

You can also extend the supported ways to custom ones, but this is out of the scope of this book.

Argo CD detects a Kustomize project if there are any of the following files: *kustomization.yaml*, *kustomization.yml*, or *Kustomization*.

Let's deploy the same BGD application, but in this case, deployed as Kustomize manifests.

Moreover, we'll set `kustomize` to override the `COLOR` environment variable to yellow.

The Kustomize file defined in the repository looks like this:

```
apiVersion: kustomize.config.k8s.io/v1beta1
kind: Kustomization
namespace: bgdk
resources:
- ../base ❶
- bgdk-ns.yaml ❷
patchesJson6902: ❸
  - target: ❹
      version: v1
      group: apps
      kind: Deployment
      name: bgd
      namespace: bgdk
    patch: |- ❺
      - op: replace
        path: /spec/template/spec/containers/0/env/0/value
        value: yellow
```

❶ Directory with standard deployment files (blue circles)

❷ Specific file for creating a namespace

❸ Patches standard deployment files

❹ Patches the deployment file

❺ Overrides the environment variable value to `yellow`

You don't need to create this file as it's already stored in the Git repository.

Create the following `Application` file to deploy the application:

```
apiVersion: argoproj.io/v1alpha1
kind: Application
metadata:
  name: bgdk-app
  namespace: argocd
spec:
  destination:
    namespace: bgdk
    server: https://kubernetes.default.svc
  project: default
  source:
    path: ch07/bgdk/bgdk
    repoURL: https://github.com/gitops-cookbook/gitops-cookbook-sc.git
```

```
    targetRevision: main
  syncPolicy:
    automated: {}
```

At this point, we can apply the `Application` file to a running cluster by running the following command:

```
kubectl apply -f bgdk/bgdk-app.yaml
```

Access the service and you'll notice the circles are yellow instead of blue.

To remove the application, use the CLI tool or the UI:

```
argocd app delete bgdk-app
```

Discussion

We can explicitly specify which tool to use, overriding the default algorithm used by Argo CD in the `Application` file. For example, we can use a plain directory strategy regarding the presence of the *kustomization.yaml* file:

```
source:
  directory: ❶
    recurse: true
```

❶ Overrides always use a plain directory strategy

Possible strategies are: `directory`, `chart`, `helm`, `kustomize`, `path`, and `plugin`.

 Everything we've seen about Kustomize is valid when using Argo CD.

See Also

- Chapter 4
- argo-cd/application-crd.yaml on GitHub (*https://oreil.ly/EIxY1*)
- Argo CD Tool Detection (*https://oreil.ly/DJbiU*)

7.4 Helm Integration

Problem

You want to use Argo CD to deploy Helm manifests.

Solution

Argo CD supports installing Helm Charts to the cluster when it detects a Helm project in the deployment directory (when the *Chart.yaml* file is present).

Let's deploy the same BGD application, but in this case, deployed as a Helm manifest.

The layout of the project is a simple Helm layout already created in the GitHub repository you've cloned previously:

```
├── Chart.yaml
├── charts
├── templates
│   ├── NOTES.txt
│   ├── _helpers.tpl
│   ├── deployment.yaml
│   ├── ns.yaml
│   ├── service.yaml
│   ├── serviceaccount.yaml
│   └── tests
│       └── test-connection.yaml
└── values.yaml
```

Create a *bgdh/bgdh-app.yaml* file to define the Argo CD application:

```yaml
apiVersion: argoproj.io/v1alpha1
kind: Application
metadata:
  name: bgdh-app
  namespace: argocd
spec:
  destination:
    namespace: bgdh
    server: https://kubernetes.default.svc
  project: default
  source:
    path: ch07/bgdh
    repoURL: https://github.com/gitops-cookbook/gitops-cookbook-sc.git
    targetRevision: main
  syncPolicy:
    automated: {}
```

At this point, we can apply the `Application` file into a running cluster by running the following command:

```
kubectl apply -f bgdh/bgdh-app.yaml
```

Validate the pod is running in the bgdh namespace:

```
kubectl get pods -n bgdh
```

```
NAME                         READY   STATUS    RESTARTS   AGE
bgdh-app-556c46fcd6-ctfkf    1/1     Running   0          5m43s
```

To remove the application, use the CLI tool or the UI:

```
argocd app delete bgdh-app
```

Discussion

Argo CD populates build environment variables to Helm manifests (actually also Kustomize, Jsonnet, and custom tools support too).

The following variables are set:

- ARGOCD_APP_NAME

- ARGOCD_APP_NAMESPACE

- ARGOCD_APP_REVISION

- ARGOCD_APP_SOURCE_PATH

- ARGOCD_APP_SOURCE_REPO_URL

- ARGOCD_APP_SOURCE_TARGET_REVISION

- KUBE_VERSION

- KUBE_API_VERSIONS

In the following snippet, you can see the usage of the application name:

```
apiVersion: argoproj.io/v1alpha1
kind: Application
metadata:
  name: bgdh-app
  namespace: openshift-gitops
spec:
  destination:
  ...
  source:
    path: ch07/bgd
    ...
    helm: ❶
      parameters: ❷
      - name: app ❸
        value: $ARGOCD_APP_NAME ❹
```

❶ Specific Helm section

❷ Extra parameters to set, same as setting them in *values.yaml*, but high preference

❸ The name of the parameter

❹ The value of the parameter, in this case from a Build Env var

Argo CD can use a different *values.yaml* file or set parameter values to override the ones defined in *values.yaml*:

```
argocd app set bgdh-app --values new-values.yaml
```

```
argocd app set bgdh-app -p service.type=LoadBalancer
```

Note that values files must be in the same Git repository as the Helm Chart.

 Argo CD supports Helm hooks too.

See Also

- Chapter 5
- *argo-cd/application-crd.yaml* on GitHub (*https://oreil.ly/EIxY1*)

7.5 Image Updater

Problem

You want Argo CD to automatically deploy a container image when it's published.

Solution

Use Argo CD Image Updater (*https://oreil.ly/kztMq*) to detect a change on the container registry and update the deployment files.

One of the most repetitive tasks during development is deploying a new version of a container image.

With a pure Argo CD solution, after the container image is published to a container registry, we need to update the Kubernetes/Kustomize/Helm manifest files pointing to the new container image and push the result to the Git repository.

This process implies:

1. Clone the repo
2. Parse the YAML files and update them accordingly
3. Commit and Push the changes

These boilerplate tasks should be defined for each repository during the continuous integration phase. Although this approach works, it could be automated so the cluster could detect a new image pushed to the container registry and update the current deployment file pointing to the newer version.

This is exactly what Argo CD Image Updater (*ArgoCD IU*) does. It's a Kubernetes controller monitoring for a new container version and updating the manifests defined in the Argo CD `Application` file.

The Argo CD IU lifecycle and its relationship with Argo CD are shown in Figure 7-6.

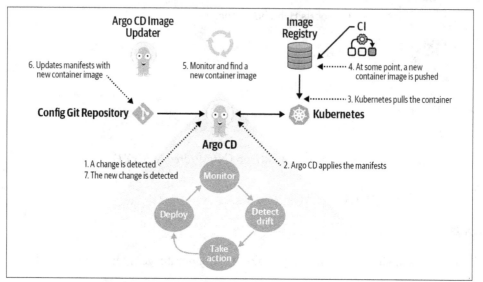

Figure 7-6. Argo CD Image Updater lifecycle

At this time, Argo CD IU only updates manifests of Kustomize or Helm. In the case of Helm, it needs to support specifying the image's tag using a parameter (`image.tag`).

Let's install the controller in the same namespace as Argo CD:

```
kubectl apply -f \
https://raw.githubusercontent.com/argoproj-labs/argocd-imageupdater/v0.12.0/mani-
fests/install.yaml -n argocd
```

Validate the installation process, checking that the pod status of the controller is `Running`:

```
kubectl get pods -n argocd

NAME                                          READY   STATUS
RESTARTS   AGE
argocd-image-updater-59c45cbc5c-kjjtp         1/1     Running
0          40h
```

Before using Argo CD IU, we create a Kubernetes Secret representing the Git credentials, so the updated manifests can be pushed to the repository. The secret must be at the Argo CD namespace and, in this case, we name it `git-creds`.

```
kubectl -n argocd create secret generic git-creds \ --from-literal=user
name=<git_user> \
--from-literal=password=<git_password_or_token>
```

Finally, let's annotate the `Application` manifest with some special annotations so the controller can start monitoring the registry:

image-list

Specify one or more images (comma-separated-value) considered for updates.

write-back-method

Methods to propagate new versions. There are `git` and `argocd` methods implemented to update to a newer image. The Git method commits the change to the Git repository. Argo CD uses the Kubernetes/ArgoCD API to update the resource.

There are more configuration options, but the previous ones are the most important to get started.

Let's create an Argo CD `Application` manifest annotated with Argo CD IU annotations:

```
apiVersion: argoproj.io/v1alpha1
kind: Application
metadata:
  name: bgdk-app
  namespace: argocd
  annotations: ❶
    argocd-image-updater.argoproj.io/image-list: myalias=quay.io/rhdevelopers/bgd
❷
    argocd-image-updater.argoproj.io/write-back-method: git:secret:openshift-
gitops/git-creds ❸
    argocd-image-updater.argoproj.io/git-branch: main ❹
spec:
  destination:
    namespace: bgdk
    server: https://kubernetes.default.svc
  project: default
  source:
    path: ch07/bgdui/bgdk
    repoURL: https://github.com/gitops-cookbook/gitops-cookbook-sc.git
    targetRevision: main
  syncPolicy:
    automated: {}
```

❶   Adds annotations section

② Sets the monitored image name

③ Configures to use Git as `write-back-method`, setting the location of the credentials (`<namespace>/<secretname>`)

④ Sets the branch to push changes

Now apply the manifest to deploy the application's first version and enable Argo CD IU to update the repository when a new image is pushed to the container registry:

```
kubectl apply -f bgdui/bgdui-app.yaml
```

At this point, version `1.0.0` is up and running in the bgdk namespace, and you may access it as we've done before. Let's generate a new container version to validate that the new image is in the repository.

To simplify the process, we'll tag the container with version `1.1.0` as it was a new one.

Go to the Quay repository created at the beginning of this chapter, go to the tags section, push the gear icon, and select `Add New Tag` to create a new container, as shown in Figure 7-7.

Figure 7-7. Tag container

Set the tag to `1.1.0` value as shown in the figure Figure 7-8.

> ### Add Tag to Manifest sha256:e0187fae04d9 ✕
>
> | 1.1.0 |
>
> **Create Tag** **Cancel**

Figure 7-8. Tag container

After this step, you should have a new container created as shown in Figure 7-9.

Wait for around two minutes until the change is detected and the controller triggers the repo update.

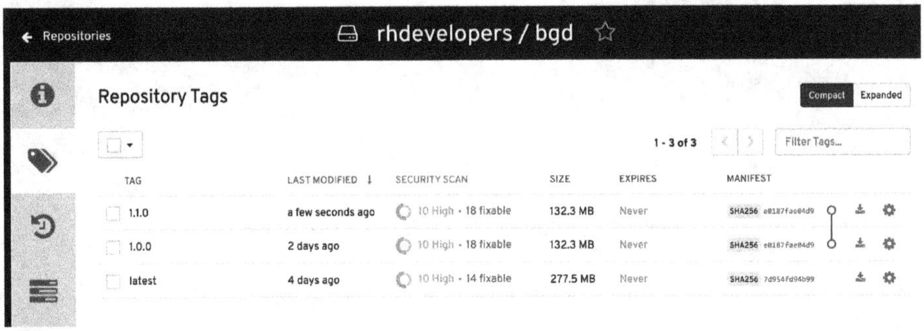

Figure 7-9. Final result

To validate the triggering process check the logs of the controller:

```
kubectl logs argocd-image-updater-59c45cbc5c-kjjtp -f -n argocd


...
time="2022-06-20T21:19:05Z" level=info msg="Setting new image to quay.io/rhdevel
opers/bgd:1.1.0" alias=myalias application=bgdk-app image_name=rhdevelopers/bgd
image_tag=1.0.0 registry=quay.io
time="2022-06-20T21:19:05Z" level=info msg="Successfully updated image 'quay.io/
rhdevelopers/bgd:1.0.0' to 'quay.io/rhdevelopers/bgd:1.1.0', but pending spec
update (dry run=false)" alias=myalias application=bgdk-app image_name=rhdevelop
ers/bgd image_tag=1.0.0 registry=quay.io ❶
time="2022-06-20T21:19:05Z" level=info msg="Committing 1 parameter update(s) for
application bgdk-app" application=bgdk-app
...
```

❶ Detects the change and updates the image

After that, if you inspect the repository, you'll see a new Kustomize file named .argocd-source-bgdk-app.yaml, updating the image value to the new container, as shown in Figure 7-10.

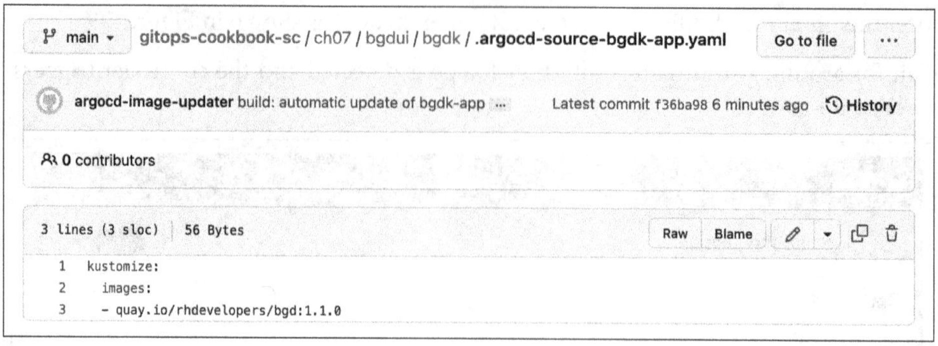

Figure 7-10. New Kustomize file updating to the new container

Now Argo CD can detect the change and update the cluster properly with the new image.

To remove the application, use the CLI tool or the UI:

```
argocd app delete bgdk-app
```

Discussion

An update strategy defines how Argo CD IU will find new versions. With no change, Argo CD IU uses a semantic version to detect the latest version.

An optional version constraint field may be added to restrict which versions are allowed to be automatically updated. To only update patch versions, we can change the image-list annotation as shown in the following snippet:

```
argocd-image-updater.argoproj.io/image-list: myalias=quay.io/rhdevelopers/bgd:1.2.x
```

Argo CD Image Updater can update to the image that has the most recent build date:

```
argocd-image-updater.argoproj.io/myalias.update-strategy: latest
argocd-image-updater.argoproj.io/myimage.allow-tags: regexp:^[0-9a-f]{7}$ ❶
```

❶ Restricts the tags considered for the update

The digest update strategy will use image digests to update your applications' image tags:

```
argocd-image-updater.argoproj.io/myalias.update-strategy: digest
```

So far, the container was stored in a public registry. If the repository is private, Argo CD Image Updater needs read access to the repo to detect any change.

First of all, create a new secret representing the container registry credentials:

```
kubectl create -n argocd secret docker-registry quayio --docker-server=quay.io --docker-username=$QUAY_USERNAME --docker-password=$QUAY_PASSWORD
```

Argo CD Image Updater uses a `ConfigMap` as a configuration source, which is the place to register the private container registry. Create a new `ConfigMap` manifest setting the supported registries:

```
apiVersion: v1
kind: ConfigMap
metadata:
  name: argocd-image-updater-config ❶
data:
  registries.conf: |
    registries: ❷
    - name: RedHat Quay ❸
      api_url: https://quay.io ❹
      prefix: quay.io ❺
      insecure: yes
      credentials: pullsecret:argocd/quayio ❻
```

❶ Name of the Argo CD IU `ConfigMap`

❷ Place to register all registries

❸ A name to identify it

❹ URL of the service

❺ The prefix used in the container images

❻ Gets the credentials from the `quayio` secret stored at `argocd` namespace

Argo CD Image Updater commits the update with a default message:

```
commit 3caf0af8b7a26de70a641c696446bbe1cd04cea8 (HEAD -> main, origin/main)
Author: argocd-image-updater <noreply@argoproj.io>
Date:   Thu Jun 23 09:41:00 2022 +0000

    build: automatic update of bgdk-app

updates image rhdevelopers/bgd tag '1.0.0' to '1.1.0'
```

We can update the default commit message to one that fits your requirements. Configure the `git.commit-message-template` key in ArgoCD IU `argocd-image-updater-config` ConfigMap with the message:

```
apiVersion: v1
kind: ConfigMap
metadata:
  name: argocd-image-updater-config ❶
data:
  git.user: alex ❷
  git.email: alex@example.com ❸
  git.commit-message-template: | ❹
```

```
build: automatic update of {{ .AppName }} ❺

{{ range .AppChanges -}} ❻
updates image {{ .Image }} tag '{{ .OldTag }}' to '{{ .NewTag }}' ❼ ❽ ❾
{{ end -}}
```

❶ Argo CD IU `ConfigMap`

❷ Commit user

❸ Commmit email

❹ Golang `text/template` content

❺ The name of the application

❻ List of changes performed by the update

❼ Image name

❽ Previous container tag

❾ New container tag

> Remember to restart the Argo CD UI controller when the `Config`
> `Map` is changed:
>
> ```
> kubectl rollout restart deployment argocd-image-updater
> -n argocd
> ```

See Also

- Argo CD Image Updater (*https://oreil.ly/kztMq*)

7.6 Deploy from a Private Git Repository

Problem

You want Argo CD to deploy manifests.

Solution

Use Argo CD CLI/UI or YAML files to register the repositories' credential information (username/password/token/key).

In Argo CD, you have two ways to register a Git repository with its credentials. One way is using the Argo CD CLI/Argo CD UI tooling. To register a private repository in Argo CD, set the username and password by running the following command:

```
argocd repo add https://github.com/argoproj/argocd-example-apps \
--username <username> --password <password>
```

Alternatively, we can use the Argo CD UI to register it too. Open Argo CD UI in a browser, and click the Settings/Repositories button (the one with gears) as shown in Figure 7-11.

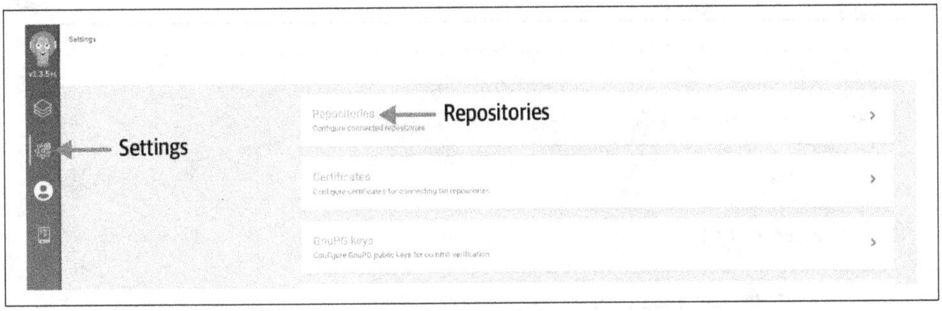

Figure 7-11. Settings menu

Then click the "Connect Repo using HTTPS" button and fill the form with the required data as shown in Figure 7-12.

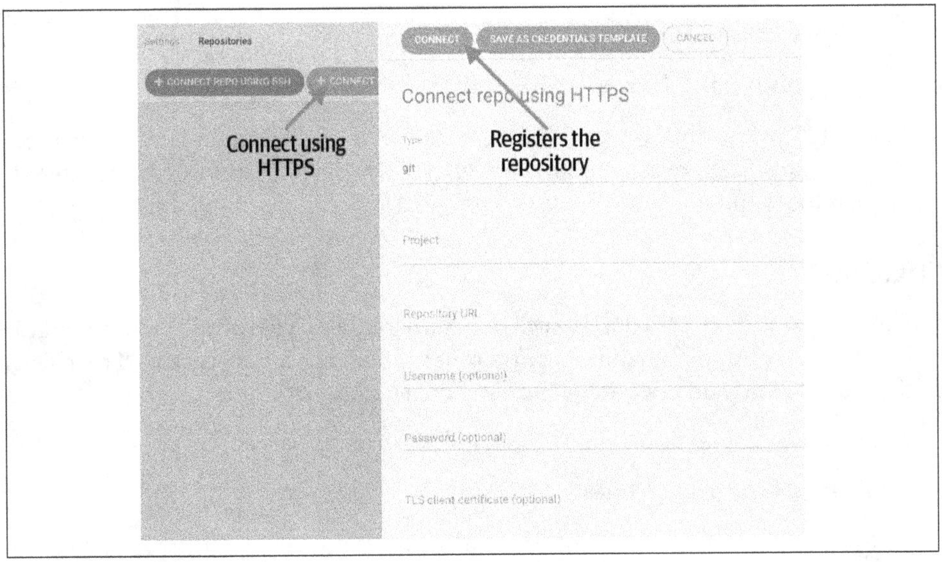

Figure 7-12. Configuration of repository

Finally, click the Connect button to test that it's possible to establish a connection and add the repository into Argo CD.

The other way is to create a Kubernetes Secret manifest file with that repository and credentials information:

```
apiVersion: v1
kind: Secret
metadata:
  name: private-repo
  namespace: argocd ❶
  labels:
     argocd.argoproj.io/secret-type: repository ❷
stringData:
  type: git
  url: https://github.com/argoproj/private-repo ❸
  password: my-password ❹
  username: my-username ❺
```

❶ Create a secret in the Argo CD namespace

❷ Sets secret type as `repository`

❸ URL of the repository to register

❹ Password to access

❺ Username to access

If you apply this file, it will have the same effect as the manual approach.

At this point, every time we define a `repoURL` value in the `Application` resource with a repository URL registered for authentication, Argo CD will use the registered credentials to log in.

Discussion

In addition to setting credentials such as username and password for accessing a private Git repo, Argo CD also supports other methods such as tokens, TLS client certificates, SSH private keys, or GitHub App credentials.

Let's see some examples using Argo CD CLI or Kubernetes Secrets.

To configure a TLS client certificate:

```
argocd repo add https://repo.example.com/repo.git \
--tls-client-cert-path ~/mycert.crt \
--tls-client-cert-key-path ~/mycert.key
```

For SSH, you just need to set the location of the SSH private key:

```
argocd repo add git@github.com:argoproj/argocd-example-apps.git \
--ssh-privatekey-path ~/.ssh/id_rsa
```

Or using a Kubernetes Secret:

```
apiVersion: v1
kind: Secret
metadata:
  name: private-repo
  namespace: argocd
  labels:
    argocd.argoproj.io/secret-type: repository
stringData:
  type: git
  url: git@github.com:argoproj/my-private-repository
  sshPrivateKey: | ❶
    -----BEGIN OPENSSH PRIVATE KEY-----
    ...
    -----END OPENSSH PRIVATE KEY-----
```

❶ Sets the content of the SSH private key

If you are using the GitHub App method, you need to set the App ID, the App Installation ID, and the private key:

```
argocd repo add https://github.com/argoproj/argocd-example-apps.git --github-app-
id 1 --github-app-installation-id 2 --github-app-private-key-path test.private-
key.pem
```

Or using the declarative approach:

```
apiVersion: v1
kind: Secret
metadata:
  name: github-repo
  namespace: argocd
  labels:
    argocd.argoproj.io/secret-type: repository
stringData:
  type: git
  repo: https://ghe.example.com/argoproj/my-private-repository
  githubAppID: 1 ❶
  githubAppInstallationID: 2
  githubAppEnterpriseBaseUrl: https://ghe.example.com/api/v3 ❷
  githubAppPrivateKeySecret: |
    -----BEGIN OPENSSH PRIVATE KEY-----
    ...
    -----END OPENSSH PRIVATE KEY-----
```

❶ Sets GitHub App parameters

❷ Only valid if GitHub App Enterprise is used

For the access token, use the account name as the username and the token in the password field.

Choosing which strategy to use will depend on your experience managing Kubernetes Secrets. Remember that a Secret in Kubernetes is not encrypted but encoded in Base64, so it is not secured by default.

We recommend using only the declarative approach when you've got a good strategy for securing the secrets.

 We've not discussed the Sealed Secrets project yet (we'll do so in the following chapter), but when using Sealed Secrets, the labels will be removed to avoid the SealedSecret object having a template section that encodes all the fields you want the controller to put in the unsealed Secret:

```
spec:
  ...
  template:
    metadata:
      labels:
        "argocd.argoproj.io/secret-type": repository
```

7.7 Order Kubernetes Manifests

Problem

You want to use Argo CD to deploy.

Solution

Use *sync waves* and *resource hooks* to modify the default order of applying manifests.

Argo CD applies the Kubernetes manifests (plain, Helm, Kustomize) in a particular order using the following logic:

1. By kind
    a. Namespaces
    b. NetworkPolicy
    c. Limit Range
    d. ServiceAccount
    e. Secret
    f. ConfigMap
    g. StorageClass

h. PersistentVolumes

i. ClusterRole

j. Role

k. Service

l. DaemonSet

m. Pod

n. ReplicaSet

o. Deployment

p. StatefulSet

q. Job

r. Ingress

2. In the same kind, then by name (alphabetical order)

Argo CD has three phases when applying resources: the first phase is executed before applying the manifests (PreSync), the second phase is when the manifests are applied (Sync), and the third phase is executed after all manifests are applied and synchronized (PostSync).

Figure 7-13 summarizes these phases.

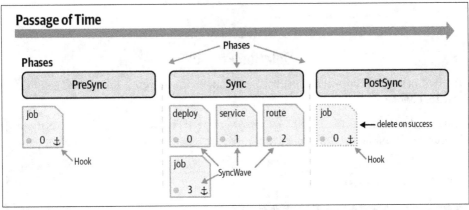

Figure 7-13. Hooks and sync waves

Resource hooks are scripts executed at a given phase, or if the Sync phase failed, you could run some rollback operations.

Table 7-1 lists the available resource hooks.

Table 7-1. Resource hooks

Hook	Description	Use case
PreSync	Executes prior to the application of the manifests	Database migrations
Sync	Executes at the same time as manifests	Complex rolling update strategies like canary releases or dark launches
PostSync	Executes after all Sync hooks have completed and were successful (healthy)	Run tests to validate deployment was correctly done
SyncFail	Executes when the sync operation fails	Rollback operations in case of failure
Skip	Skip the application of the manifest	When manual steps are required to deploy the application (i.e., releasing public traffic to new version)

Hooks are defined as an annotation named `argocd.argoproj.io/hook` to a Kubernetes resource. In the following snippet, a `PostSync` manifest is defined:

```
apiVersion: batch/v1
kind: Job
metadata:
  name: todo-insert ❶
  annotations:
    argocd.argoproj.io/hook: PostSync ❷
```

❶ Job's name

❷ Sets when the manifest is applied

Deletion Policies

A hook is not deleted when finished; for example, if you run a Kubernetes Job, it'll remain `Completed`.

This might be the desired state, but we can specify to automatically delete these resources if annotated with `argocd.argoproj.io/hook-delete-policy` and the policy value is set.

Supported policies are:

Policy	Description
HookSucceeded	Deleted after the hook succeeded
HookFailed	Deleted after the hook failed
BeforeHookCreation	Deleted before the new one is created

A *sync wave* is a way to order how Argo CD applies the manifests stored in Git.

All manifests have zero waves by default, and the lower values go first. Use the `argocd.argoproj.io/sync-wave` annotation to set the wave number to a resource.

For example, you might want to deploy a database first and then create the database schema; for this case, you should set a `sync-wave` lower in the database deployment file than in the job for creating the database schema, as shown in the following snippet:

```
apiVersion: apps/v1
kind: Deployment
metadata:
  name: postgresql ❶
  namespace: todo
  annotations:
    argocd.argoproj.io/sync-wave: "0" ❷
...
apiVersion: batch/v1
kind: Job
metadata:
  name: todo-table ❸
  namespace: todo
  annotations:
    argocd.argoproj.io/sync-wave: "1" ❹
```

❶ PostgreSQL deployment

❷ Sync wave for PostgreSQL deployment is 0

❸ Name of the Job

❹ Job executed when PostgreSQL is healthy

Discussion

When Argo CD starts applying the manifests, it orders the resources in the following way:

1. Phase
2. Wave (lower precedence first)
3. Kind
4. Name

Let's deploy a more significant application with deployment files, sync waves, and hooks.

The sample application deployed is a TODO application connected with a database (PostgreSQL) to store TODOs. To deploy the application, some particular order needs to be applied; for example, the database server must be running before creating the database schema. Also, when the whole application is deployed, we insert some default TODOs into the database to run a post-sync manifest.

The overall process is shown in Figure 7-14.

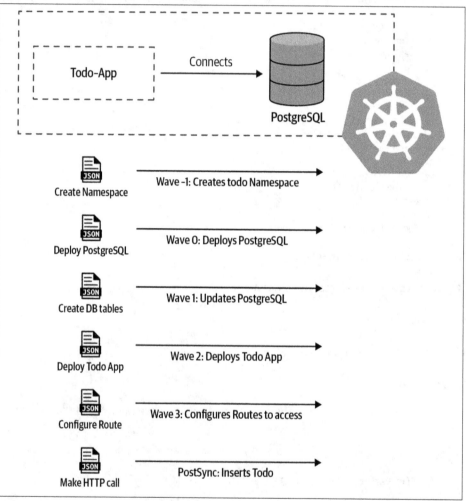

Figure 7-14. Todo app

Create an `Application` resource pointing out to the application:

```
apiVersion: argoproj.io/v1alpha1
kind: Application
metadata:
  name: todo-app
  namespace: argocd
spec:
  destination:
    namespace: todo
    server: https://kubernetes.default.svc
  project: default
  source:
    path: ch07/todo
    repoURL: https://github.com/gitops-cookbook/gitops-cookbook-sc.git
    targetRevision: main
  syncPolicy:
    automated:
      prune: true
      selfHeal: false
    syncOptions:
    - CreateNamespace=true
```

In the terminal, apply the resource, and Argo CD will deploy all applications in the specified order.

See Also

- *gitops-engine/sync_tasks.go* on GitHub (*https://oreil.ly/NDWru*)

7.8 Define Synchronization Windows

Problem

You want Argo CD to block or allow application synchronization depending on time.

Solution

Argo CD has the *sync windows* concept to configure time windows where application synchronizations (applying new resources that have been pushed to the repository) will either be blocked or allowed.

To define a sync window, create an `AppProject` manifest setting the `kind` (either `allow` or `deny`), a `schedule` in cron format to define the initial time, a `duration` of the window, and which resources the sync window is applied to (`Application`, namespaces, or clusters).

About Cron Expressions

A cron expression represents a time. It's composed of the following fields:

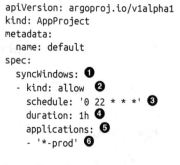

```
┌───────────── minute (0 - 59)
│ ┌─────────── hour (0 - 23)
│ │ ┌───────── day of the month (1 - 31)
│ │ │ ┌─────── month (1 - 12)
│ │ │ │ ┌───── day of the week (0 - 6)
* * * * *
```

The `AppProject` resource is responsible for defining these windows where synchronizations are permitted/blocked.

Create a new file to permit synchronizations only from 22:00 to 23:00 (just one hour) and for Argo CD `Applications` whose names end in `-prod`:

```
apiVersion: argoproj.io/v1alpha1
kind: AppProject
metadata:
  name: default
spec:
  syncWindows: ❶
  - kind: allow ❷
    schedule: '0 22 * * *' ❸
    duration: 1h ❹
    applications: ❺
    - '*-prod' ❻
```

❶ List of windows

❷ Allow syncs

❸ Only at 22:00

❹ For 1 hour (23:00)

❺ Sets the applications that affect this window

❻ Regular expression matching any application whose name ends with `-prod`

Discussion

We cannot perform a sync of the application (neither automatic nor manual) when it's not the time configured in the time window defined in the `AppProject` manifest. However, we can configure a window to allow manual syncs.

Using the CLI tool:

```
argocd proj windows enable-manual-sync <PROJECT ID>
```

Also, manual sync can be set in the YAML file. In the following example, we're setting manual synchronization for the `namespace` default, denying synchronizations at 22:00 for one hour and allowing synchronizations in `prod-cluster` at 23:00 for one hour:

```
apiVersion: argoproj.io/v1alpha1
kind: AppProject
metadata:
  name: default
  namespace: argocd
spec:
  syncWindows:
  - kind: deny ❶
    schedule: '0 22 * * *'
    duration: 1h
    manualSync: true ❷
    namespaces: ❸
    - bgd
  - kind: allow
    schedule: '0 23 * * *'
    duration: 1h
    clusters: ❹
    - prod-cluster
```

❶ Block synchronizations

❷ Enable manual sync to `default` namespace

❸ Configure namespaces to block

❹ Configure clusters to allow syncs at 23:00

We can inspect the current windows from the UI by going to the Settings → Projects → default → windows tab or by using the `argocd` CLI tool:

```
argocd proj windows list default
```

```
ID  STATUS    KIND   SCHEDULE    DURATION  APPLICATIONS  NAMESPACES  CLUSTERS
MANUALSYNC
0   Inactive  deny   0 22 * * *  1h        -             bgd         -
Enabled
1   Inactive  allow  0 23 * * *  1h        -             -           prod-cluster
Disabled
```

## CHAPTER 8

Advanced Topics

In the previous chapter, you had an overview of implementing GitOps workflows using Argo CD recipes. Argo CD is a famous and influential open source project that helps with both simple use cases and more advanced ones. In this chapter, we will discuss topics needed when you move forward in your GitOps journey, and you need to manage security, automation, and advanced deployment models for multicluster scenarios.

Security is a critical aspect of automation and DevOps. DevSecOps is a new definition of an approach where security is a shared responsibility throughout the entire IT life-cycle. Furthermore, the DevSecOps Manifesto (*https://www.devsecops.org*) specifies security as code to operate and contribute value with less friction. And this goes in the same direction as GitOps principles, where everything is declarative.

On the other hand, this also poses the question of avoiding storing unencrypted plain-text credentials in Git. As stated in the book *Path to GitOps* by Christian Hernandez, Argo CD luckily currently provides two patterns to manage security in GitOps workflows:

- Storing encrypted secrets in Git, such as with a Sealed Secret (see Recipe 8.1)
- Storing secrets in external services or vaults, then storing only the reference to such secrets in Git (see Recipe 8.2)

The chapter then moves to advanced deployment techniques, showing how to manage webhooks with Argo CD (see Recipe 8.3) and with ApplicationSets (see Recipe 8.4). ApplicationSets is a component of Argo CD that allows management deployments of many applications, repositories, or clusters from a single Kubernetes resource. In essence, a templating system for the GitOps application is ready to be deployed and synced in multiple Kubernetes clusters (see Recipe 8.5).

Last but not least, the book ends with a recipe on Progressive Delivery for Kubernetes with Argo Rollouts (Recipe 8.6), useful for deploying the application using an advanced deployment technique such as blue-green or canary.

8.1 Encrypt Sensitive Data (Sealed Secrets)

Problem

You want to manage Kubernetes Secrets and encrypted objects in Git.

Solution

Sealed Secrets (*https://oreil.ly/MWTNB*) is an open source project by Bitnami used to encrypt a Kubernetes Secrets into a SealedSecret Kubernetes Custom Resource, representing an encrypted object safe to store in Git.

Sealed Secrets uses public-key cryptography and consists of two main components:

- A Kubernetes controller that has knowledge about the private and public key used to decrypt and encrypt encrypted secrets and is responsible for reconciliation. The controller also supports automatic secret rotation for the private key and key expiration management in order to enforce the re-encryption of secrets.

- kubeseal, a CLI used by developers to encrypt their secrets before committing them to a Git repository.

The SealedSecret object is encrypted and decrypted only by the SealedSecret controller running in the target Kubernetes cluster. This operation is exclusive only to this component, thus nobody else can decrypt the object. The kubeseal CLI allows the developer to take a normal Kubernetes Secret resource and convert it to a SealedSecret resource definition as shown in Figure 8-1.

In your Kubernetes cluster with Argo CD, you can install the kubeseal CLI for your operating system from the GitHub project's releases (*https://oreil.ly/zmEh3*). At the time of writing this book, we are using version 0.18.2.

On macOS, kubeseal is available through Homebrew (*https://brew.sh*) as follows:

```
brew install kubeseal
```

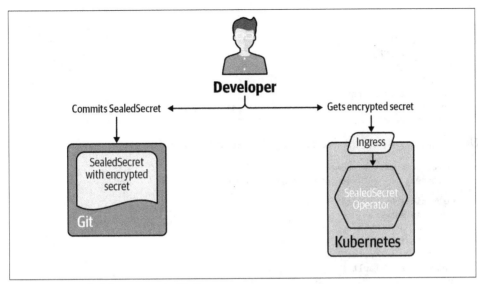

Figure 8-1. Sealed Secrets with GitOps

After you install the CLI, you can install the controller as follows:

```
kubectl create \
-f https://github.com/bitnami-labs/sealed-secrets/releases/download/0.18.2/control-
ler.yaml
```

You should have output similar to the following:

```
serviceaccount/sealed-secrets-controller created
deployment.apps/sealed-secrets-controller created
customresourcedefinition.apiextensions.k8s.io/sealedsecrets.bitnami.com created
service/sealed-secrets-controller created
rolebinding.rbac.authorization.k8s.io/sealed-secrets-controller created
rolebinding.rbac.authorization.k8s.io/sealed-secrets-service-proxier created
role.rbac.authorization.k8s.io/sealed-secrets-service-proxier created
role.rbac.authorization.k8s.io/sealed-secrets-key-admin created
clusterrolebinding.rbac.authorization.k8s.io/sealed-secrets-controller created
clusterrole.rbac.authorization.k8s.io/secrets-unsealer created
```

As an example, let's create a Secret for the Pac-Man game deployed in Chapter 5:

```
kubectl create secret generic pacman-secret \
--from-literal=user=pacman \
--from-literal=pass=pacman
```

You should have the following output:

```
secret/pacman-secret created
```

And here you can see the YAML representation:

```
kubectl get secret pacman-secret  -o yaml
```

```
apiVersion: v1
data:
  pass: cGFjbWFu
  user: cGFjbWFu
kind: Secret
metadata:
  name: pacman-secret
  namespace: default
type: Opaque
```

Now, you can convert the Secret into a `SealedSecret` in this way:

```
kubectl get secret pacman-secret -o yaml \
| kubeseal -o yaml > pacman-sealedsecret.yaml
```

```
apiVersion: bitnami.com/v1alpha1
kind: SealedSecret
metadata:
  creationTimestamp: null
  name: pacman-secret
  namespace: default
spec:
  encryptedData: ❶
    pass: AgBJR1AgZ5Gu5NOVsG1E8SKBcdB3QSDdzZka3RRYuWV7z8g7ccQ0dGc1suVOP8wX/
ZpPmIMp8+urPYG62k4EZRUjuu/Vg2E1nSbsGBh9eKu3NaO6tGSF3eGk6PzN6XtRhDeER4u7MG5pj/
+FXRAKcy8Z6RfzbVEGq/QJQ4z0ecSNdJmG07ERMm1Q+lPNGvph2Svx8aCgFLqRsdLhFyvwb
TyB3XnmFHrPr+2DynxeN8XVMoMkRYXgVc6GAoxUK7CnC3Elpuy7lIdPwc5QBx9kUVfra83LX8/KxeaJ
wyCqvscIGjtcxUtpTpF5jm1t1DSRRNbc4m+7pTwTmnRiUuaMVeujaBco4521yTkh5iEPjnj
vUt+VzK01NVoeNunqIazp15rFwTvmiQ5PAtbiUXpT733zCr60QBgSxPg31vw98+u+RcIHvaMIoDCqaX
xUdcn2JkUF+bZXtxNmIRTAiQVQ1vEPmrZxpvZcUh/PPC4L/RFWrQWnOzKRyqLq9wRoSLPbKyvMX
naxH0v3USGIktmtJlGjlXoW/i+HIoSeMFS0mUAzOF5M5gweOhtxKGh3Y74ZDn5PbVA/
9kbkuWgvPNGDZL924Dm6AyM5goHECr/RRTm1e22K9BfPASARZuGA6paqb9h1XEqyqesZgM0R8PLiy
Luu+tpqydR0SiYLc5VltdjzpIyyy9Xmw6Aa3/4SB+4tSwXSUUrB5yc=
    user: AgBhYDZQzOwinetPceZL897aibTYp4QPGFvP6ZhDyuUAx
OWXBQ7jBA3KPUqLvP8vBcxLAcS7HpKcDSgCdi47D2WhShdBR4jWJufwKmR3j+ayTdw72t3ALpQhTYI0iMY
TiNdR0/o3vf0jeNMt/oWCRsifqBxZaIShE53rAFEjEA6D7CuCDXu8BHk1DpSr79d5Au4puzpH
VODh+v1T+Yef3k7DUoSnbYEh3CvuRweiuq5lY8G0oob28j38wdyxm3GIrexa+M/
ZId01hxZ6jz4edv6ejdZfmQNdru3c6lmljWwcO+0Ue0MqFi4ZF/YNUsiojI+781n1m3K/
giKcyPLn0skD7DyeKPoukoN6W5P71OuFSkF+VgIeejDaxuA7bK3PEaUgv79KFC9aEEnBr/
7op7HY7X6aMDahmLUc/+zDhfzQvwnC2wcj4B8M2OBFa2ic2PmGzrIWhlBbs1OgnpehtG
SETq+YRDH0alWOdFBq1U8qn6QA8Iw6ewu8GTele3zlPLaADi5O6LrJbIZNlY0+PutWfjs9ScVVEJy+I9BGd
yT6tiA/4v4cxH6ygG6NzWkqxSaYyNrWWXtLhOlqyCpTZ
tUwHnF+OLB3gCpDZPx+NwTe2Kn0jY0c83LuLh5PJ090AsWWqZaRQyE
LeL6y6mVekQFWHGfK6t57Vb7Z3+5XJCgQn+xFLkj3SIz0ME5D4+DSsUDS1fyL8uI=
  template:
    data: null
    metadata:
      creationTimestamp: null
      name: pacman-secret
      namespace: default
    type: Opaque
```

❶ Here you find the data encrypted by the Sealed Secrets controller.

Now you can safely push your `SealedSecret` to your Kubernetes manifests repo and create the Argo CD application. Here's an example from this book's repository (*https://oreil.ly/TXHRa*):

```
argocd app create pacman \
--repo https://github.com/gitops-cookbook/pacman-kikd-manifests.git \
--path 'k8s/sealedsecrets' \
--dest-server https://kubernetes.default.svc \
--dest-namespace default \
--sync-policy auto
```

Check if the app is running and healthy:

```
argocd app list
```

You should get output similar to the following:

```
NAME     CLUSTER                      NAMESPACE  PROJECT  STATUS  HEALTH ↳
 SYNCPOLICY  CONDITIONS
REPO                                                     PATH TARGET
pacman  https://kubernetes.default.svc  default    default  Synced  Healthy↳
 <none>      <none>         https://github.com/gitops-cookbook/pacman-kikd-
manifests.git  k8s/sealedsecrets
```

8.2 Encrypt Secrets with ArgoCD (ArgoCD + HashiCorp Vault + External Secret)

Problem

You want to avoid storing credentials in Git and you want to manage them in external services or vaults.

Solution

In Recipe 8.1 you saw how to manage encrypted data in Git following the GitOps declarative way, but how do you avoid storing even encrypted credentials with GitOps?

One solution is External Secrets (*https://oreil.ly/ytBeU*), an open source project initially created by GoDaddy, which aims at storing secrets in external services or vaults from different vendors, then storing only the reference to such secrets in Git.

Today, External Secrets supports systems such as AWS Secrets Manager, HashiCorp Vault, Google Secrets Manager, Azure Key Vault, and more. The idea is to provide a user-friendly abstraction for the external API that stores and manages the lifecycles of the secrets.

In depth, ExternalSecrets is a Kubernetes controller that reconciles Secrets into the cluster from a Custom Resource that includes a reference to a secret in an external key management system. The Custom Resource `SecretStore` specifies the backend containing the confidential data, and how it should be transformed into a Secret by defining a template, as you can see in Figure 8-2. The SecretStore has the configuration to connect to the external secret manager.

Thus, the `ExternalSecrets` objects can be safely stored in Git, as they do not contain any confidential information, but just the references to the external services managing credentials.

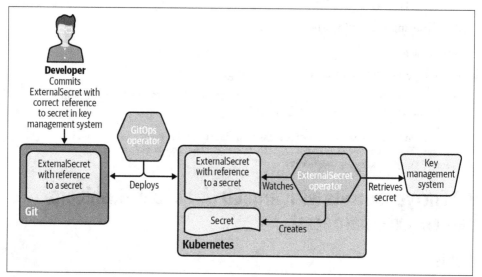

Figure 8-2. External Secrets with Argo CD

You can install External Secrets with a Helm Chart as follows. At the time of writing this book, we are using version 0.5.9:

```
helm repo add external-secrets https://charts.external-secrets.io

helm install external-secrets \
  external-secrets/external-secrets \
  -n external-secrets \
  --create-namespace
```

You should get output similar to the following:

```
NAME: external-secrets
LAST DEPLOYED: Fri Sep  2 13:09:53 2022
NAMESPACE: external-secrets
STATUS: deployed
REVISION: 1
TEST SUITE: None
NOTES:
external-secrets has been deployed successfully!
```

In order to begin using ExternalSecrets, you will need to set up a SecretStore or ClusterSecretStore resource (for example, by creating a *vault* SecretStore).

More information on the different types of SecretStores and how to configure them can be found in our GitHub page (*https://oreil.ly/LQzEh*).

 You can also install the External Secrets Operator with OLM from OperatorHub.io (*https://oreil.ly/w3x71*).

As an example with one of the providers supported, such as HashiCorp Vault (*https://oreil.ly/sg7yS*), you can do the following.

First download and install HashiCorp Vault (*https://oreil.ly/vjGSq*) for your operating system and get your Vault Token (*https://oreil.ly/6Y5cS*). Then create a Kubernetes Secret as follows:

```
export VAULT_TOKEN=<YOUR_TOKEN>
kubectl create secret generic vault-token \
  --from-literal=token=$VAULT_TOKEN \
  -n external-secrets
```

Then create a `SecretStore` as a reference to this external system:

```
apiVersion: external-secrets.io/v1beta1
kind: SecretStore
metadata:
  name: vault-secretstore
  namespace: default
spec:
  provider:
    vault:
      server: "http://vault.local:8200"  ❶
      path: "secret"
      version: "v2"
      auth:
        tokenSecretRef:
          name: "vault-token"  ❷
          key: "token"  ❸
          namespace: external-secrets
```

❶ Hostname where your Vault is running

❷ Name of the Kubernetes Secret containing the vault token

❸ Key to address the value in the Kubernetes Secret containing the vault token content:

```
kubectl create -f vault-secretstore.yaml
```

Now you can create a Secret in your Vault as follows:

```
vault kv put secret/pacman-secrets pass=pacman
```

And then reference it from the ExternalSecret as follows:

```
apiVersion: external-secrets.io/v1beta1
kind: ExternalSecret
metadata:
  name: pacman-externalsecrets
  namespace: default
spec:
  refreshInterval: "15s"
  secretStoreRef:
    name: vault-secretstore
    kind: SecretStore
  target:
    name: pacman-externalsecrets
  data:
  - secretKey: token
    remoteRef:
      key: secret/pacman-secrets
      property: pass
```

```
kubectl create -f pacman-externalsecrets.yaml
```

Now you can deploy the Pac-Man game with Argo CD using External Secrets as follows:

```
argocd app create pacman \
--repo https://github.com/gitops-cookbook/pacman-kikd-manifests.git \
--path 'k8s/externalsecrets' \
--dest-server https://kubernetes.default.svc \
--dest-namespace default \
--sync-policy auto
```

8.3 Trigger the Deployment of an Application Automatically (Argo CD Webhooks)

Problem

You don't want to wait for Argo CD syncs and you want to immediately deploy an application when a change occurs in Git.

Solution

While Argo CD polls Git repositories every three minutes to detect changes to the monitored Kubernetes manifests, it also supports an event-driven approach with webhooks notifications from popular Git servers such as GitHub, GitLab, or Bitbucket.

Argo CD Webhooks (*https://oreil.ly/3Ab46*) are enabled in your Argo CD installation and available at the endpoint /api/webhooks.

To test webhooks with Argo CD using Minikube you can use Helm to install a local Git server such as Gitea (*https://docs.gitea.io*), an open source lightweight server written in Go, as follows:

```
helm repo add gitea-charts https://dl.gitea.io/charts/
helm install gitea gitea-charts/gitea
```

You should have output similar to the following:

```
helm install gitea gitea-charts/gitea
"gitea-charts" has been added to your repositories
NAME: gitea
LAST DEPLOYED: Fri Sep  2 15:04:04 2022
NAMESPACE: default
STATUS: deployed
REVISION: 1
NOTES:
1. Get the application URL by running these commands:
   echo "Visit http://127.0.0.1:3000 to use your application"
   kubectl --namespace default port-forward svc/gitea-http 3000:3000
```

 Log in to the Gitea server with the default credentials you find the in the *values.yaml* file from the Helm Chart here (*https://oreil.ly/Nkaeu*) or define new ones via overriding them.

Import the Pac-Man (*https://oreil.ly/LwTaC*) manifests repo into Gitea.

Configure the Argo app:

```
argocd app create pacman-webhook \
--repo http://gitea-http.default.svc:3000/gitea_admin/pacman-kikd-manifests.git \
--dest-server https://kubernetes.default.svc \
--dest-namespace default \
--path k8s \
--sync-policy auto
```

To add a webhook to Gitea, navigate to the top-right corner and click Settings. Select the Webhooks tab and configure it as shown in Figure 8-3:

- Payload URL: http://localhost:9090/api/webhooks
- Content type: application/json

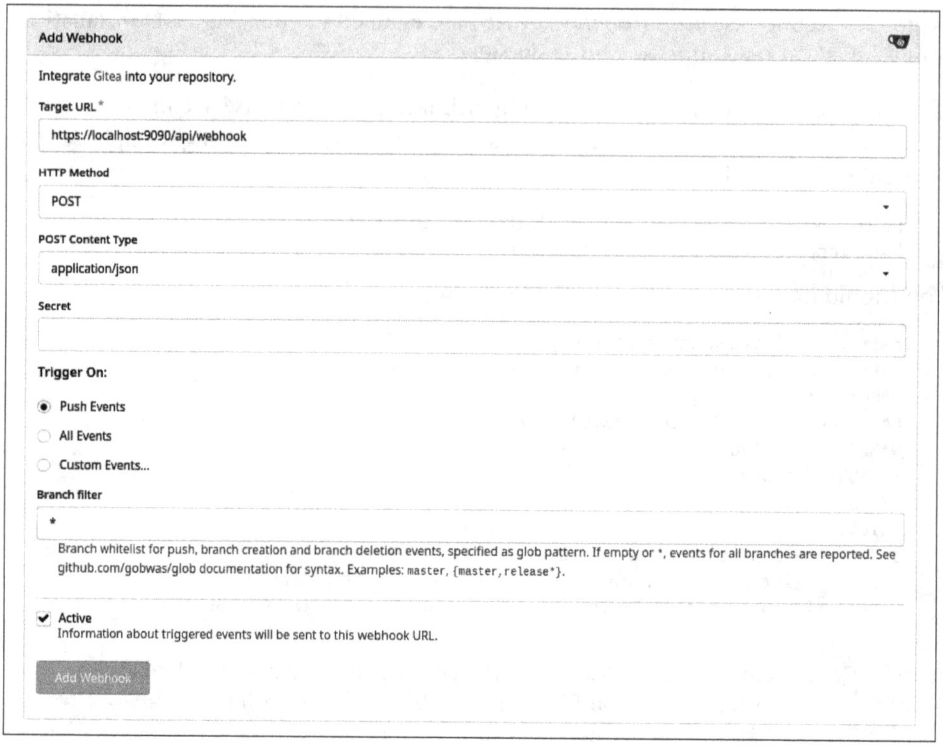

Figure 8-3. Gitea Webhooks

> You can omit the Secret for this example; however, it's best practice to configure secrets for your webhooks. Read more from the docs (*https://oreil.ly/udDkS*).

Save it and push your change to the repo on Gitea. You will see a new sync from Argo CD immediately after your push.

8.4 Deploy to Multiple Clusters

Problem

You want to deploy an application to different clusters.

Solution

Argo CD supports the ApplicationSet resource to "templetarize" an Argo CD Application resource. It covers different use cases, but the most important are:

- Use a Kubernetes manifest to target multiple Kubernetes clusters.

- Deploy multiple applications from one or multiple Git repositories.

Since the `ApplicationSet` is a template file with placeholders to substitute at runtime, we need to feed these with some values. For this purpose, `ApplicationSet` has the concept of *generators*.

A generator is responsible for generating the parameters, which will finally be replaced in the template placeholders to generate a valid Argo CD `Application`.

Create the following `ApplicationSet`:

```yaml
apiVersion: argoproj.io/v1alpha1
kind: ApplicationSet
metadata:
  name: bgd-app
  namespace: argocd
spec:
  generators: ❶
  - list:
      elements: ❷
      - cluster: staging
        url: https://kubernetes.default.svc
        location: default
      - cluster: prod
        url: https://kubernetes.default.svc
        location: app
  template: ❸
    metadata:
      name: '{{cluster}}-app' ❹
    spec:
      project: default
      source:
        repoURL: https://github.com/gitops-cookbook/gitops-cookbook-sc.git
        targetRevision: main
        path: ch08/bgd-gen/{{cluster}}
      destination:
        server: '{{url}}' ❺
        namespace: '{{location}}'
      syncPolicy:
        syncOptions:
        - CreateNamespace=true
```

❶ Defines a generator

❷ Sets the value of the parameters

❸ Defines the `Application` resource as a template

❹ `cluster` placeholder

❺ `url` placeholder

Apply the previous file by running the following command:

```
kubectl apply -f bgd-application-set.yaml
```

When this `ApplicationSet` is applied to the cluster, Argo CD generates and automatically registers two `Application` resources. The first one is:

```
apiVersion: argoproj.io/v1alpha1
kind: Application
metadata:
  name: staging-app
spec:
  project: default
  source:
    path: ch08/bgd-gen/staging
    repoURL: https://github.com/example/app.git
    targetRevision: HEAD
  destination:
    namespace: default
    server: https://kubernetes.default.svc
    ...
```

And the second one:

```
apiVersion: argoproj.io/v1alpha1
kind: Application
metadata:
  name: prod-app
spec:
  project: default
  source:
    path: ch08/bgd-gen/prod
    repoURL: https://github.com/example/app.git
    targetRevision: HEAD
  destination:
    namespace: app
    server: https://kubernetes.default.svc
    ...
```

Inspect the creation of both `Application` resources by running the following command:

```
# Remember to login first
argocd login --insecure --grpc-web $argoURL  --username admin --password $argoPass

argocd app list
```

And the output should be similar to (trunked):

```
NAME         CLUSTER                         NAMESPACE
prod-app     https://kubernetes.default.svc  app
staging-app  https://kubernetes.default.svc  default
```

Delete both applications by deleting the `ApplicationSet` file:

```
kubectl delete -f bgd-application-set.yaml
```

Discussion

We've seen the simplest generator, but there are eight generators in total at the time of writing this book:

List

Generates `Application` definitions through a fixed list of clusters. (It's the one we've seen previously).

Cluster

Similar to *List* but based on the list of clusters defined in Argo CD.

Git

Generates `Application` definitions based on a JSON/YAML properties file within a Git repository or based on the directory layout of the repository.

SCM Provider

Generates `Application` definitions from repositories within an organization.

Pull Request

Generates `Application` definitions from open pull requests.

Cluster Decision Resource

Generates `Application` definitions using duck-typing (*https://oreil.ly/kpRkV*).

Matrix

Combines values of two separate generators.

Merge

Merges values from two or more generators.

In the previous example, we created the `Application` objects from a fixed list of elements. This is fine when the number of configurable environments is small; in the example, two clusters refer to two Git folders (`ch08/bgd-gen/staging` and `ch08/bgd-gen/prod`). In the case of multiple environments (which means various folders), we can dynamically use the *Git* generator to generate one `Application` per directory.

Let's migrate the previous example to use the Git generator. As a reminder, the Git directory layout used was:

```
bgd-gen
├── staging
│   ├── ...yaml
└── prod
    ├── ...yaml
```

Create a new file of type `ApplicationSet` generating an `Application` for each directory of the configured Git repo:

```
apiVersion: argoproj.io/v1alpha1
kind: ApplicationSet
metadata:
  name: cluster-addons
  namespace: openshift-gitops
spec:
  generators:
  - git: ❶
      repoURL: https://github.com/gitops-cookbook/gitops-cookbook-sc.git
      revision: main
      directories:
      - path: ch08/bgd-gen/* ❷
    template: ❸
      metadata:
        name: '{{path[0]}}{{path[2]}}' ❹
      spec:
        project: default
        source:
          repoURL: https://github.com/gitops-cookbook/gitops-cookbook-sc.git
          targetRevision: main
          path: '{{path}}' ❺
        destination:
          server: https://kubernetes.default.svc
          namespace: '{{path.basename}}' ❻
```

❶ Configures the Git repository to read layout

❷ Initial path to start scanning directories

❸ Application definition

❹ The directory paths within the Git repository matching the path wildcard (stag ing or prod)

❺ Directory path (full path)

❻ The rightmost pathname

Apply the resource:

```
kubectl apply -f bgd-git-application-set.yaml
```

Argo CD creates two applications as there are two directories:

```
argocd app list
```

```
NAME         CLUSTER                            NAMESPACE
ch08prod     https://kubernetes.default.svc     prod
ch08staging  https://kubernetes.default.svc     staging
```

Also, this generator is handy when your application is composed of different components (service, database, distributed cache, email server, etc.), and deployment files for each element are placed in other directories. Or, for example, a repository with all operators required to be installed in the cluster:

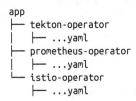

```
app
├── tekton-operator
│   ├── ...yaml
├── prometheus-operator
│   ├── ...yaml
└── istio-operator
    ├── ...yaml
```

Instead of reacting to directories, Git generator can create `Application` objects with parameters specified in JSON/YAML files.

The following snippet shows an example JSON file:

```
{
  "cluster": {
    "name": "staging",
    "address": "https://1.2.3.4"
  }
}
```

This is an excerpt of the `ApplicationSet` to react to these files:

```
apiVersion: argoproj.io/v1alpha1
kind: ApplicationSet
metadata:
  name: guestbook
spec:
  generators:
  - git:
      repoURL: https://github.com/example/app.git
      revision: HEAD
      files:
      - path: "app/**/config.json"   ❶
  template:
    metadata:
      name: '{{cluster.name}}-app'   ❷
  ....
```

❶ Finds all *config.json* files placed in all subdirectories of the `app`

❷ Injects the value set in *config.json*

This `ApplicationSet` will generate one `Application` for each *config.json* file in the folders matching the `path` expression.

See Also

- Argo CD Generators (*https://oreil.ly/EnOfl*)
- Duck Types (*https://oreil.ly/tEFQW*)

8.5 Deploy a Pull Request to a Cluster

Problem

You want to deploy a preview of the application when a pull request is created.

Solution

Use the *pull request* generator to automatically discover open pull requests within a repository and create an `Application` object.

Let's create an `ApplicationSet` reacting to any GitHub pull request annotated with the `preview` label created on the configured repository.

Create a new file named *bgd-pr-application-set.yaml* with the following content:

```
apiVersion: argoproj.io/v1alpha1
kind: ApplicationSet
metadata:
  name: myapps
  namespace: openshift-gitops
spec:
  generators:
  - pullRequest:
      github: ❶
        owner: gitops-cookbook ❷
        repo: gitops-cookbook-sc ❸
        labels: ❹
        - preview
      requeueAfterSeconds: 60 ❺
  template:
    metadata:
      name: 'myapp-{{branch}}-{{number}}' ❻
    spec:
      source:
        repoURL: 'https://github.com/gitops-cookbook/gitops-cookbook-sc.git'
        targetRevision: '{{head_sha}}' ❼
        path: ch08/bgd-pr
      project: default
      destination:
        server: https://kubernetes.default.svc
        namespace: '{{branch}}-{{number}}'
```

❶ GitHub pull request generator

---

❷ Organization/user

❸ Repository

❹ Select the target PRs

❺ Polling time in seconds to check if there is a new PR (60 seconds)

❻ Sets the name with branch name and number

❼ Sets the Git SHA number

Apply the previous file by running the following command:

```
kubectl apply -f bgd-pr-application-set.yaml
```

Now, if you list the Argo CD applications, you'll see that none are registered. The reason is there is no pull request yet in the repository labeled with `preview`:

```
argocd app list
NAME  CLUSTER  NAMESPACE  PROJECT  STATUS
```

Create a pull request against the repository and label it with `preview`.

In GitHub, the pull request window should be similar to Fjgure 8-4.

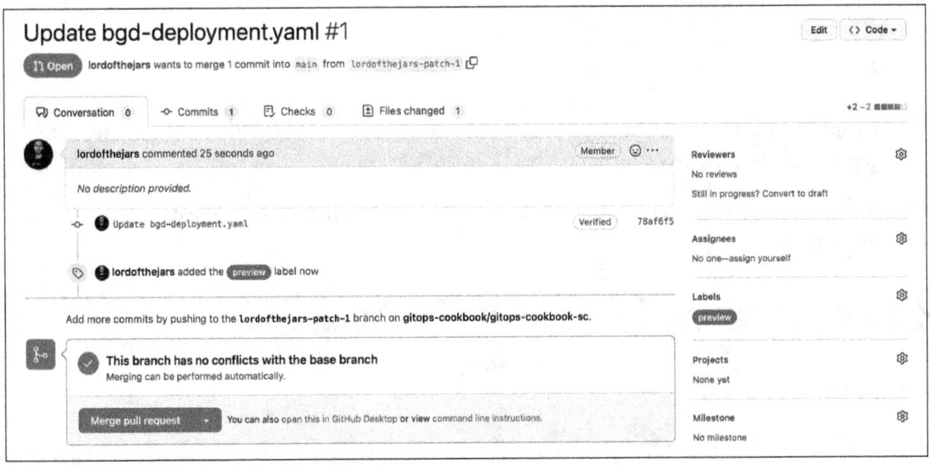

Figure 8-4. Pull request in GitHub

Wait for one minute until the `ApplicationSet` detects the change and creates the `Application` object.

Run the following command to inspect that the change has been detected and registered:

```
kubectl describe applicationset myapps -n argocd

...
Events:
  Type    Reason     Age               From                    Message
  ----    ------     ----              ----                    -------
  Normal  created    23s               applicationset-controller  created Applica-
tion "myapp-lordofthejars-patch-1-1"
  Normal  unchanged  23s (x2 over 23s) applicationset-controller  unchanged Appli-
cation "myapp-lordofthejars-patch-1-1"
```

Check the registration of the `Application` to the pull request:

```
argocd app list
NAME                            CLUSTER                      NAMESPACE
myapp-lordofthejars-patch-1-1   https://kubernetes.default.svc  lordofthejars-
patch-1-1
```

The `Application` object is automatically removed when the pull request is closed.

Discussion

At the time of writing this book, the following pull request providers are supported:

- GitHub
- Bitbucket
- Gitea
- GitLab

The ApplicationSet controller polls every `requeueAfterSeconds` interval to detect changes but also supports using webhook events.

To configure it, follow Recipe 8.3, but also enable sending pull requests events too in the Git provider.

8.6 Use Advanced Deployment Techniques

Problem

You want to deploy the application using an advanced deployment technique such as blue-green or canary.

Solution

Use the Argo Rollouts (*https://oreil.ly/g4mlf*) project to roll out updates to an application.

Argo Rollouts is a Kubernetes controller providing advanced deployment techniques such as blue-green, canary, mirroring, dark canaries, traffic analysis, etc. to Kubernetes. It integrates with many Kubernetes projects like Ambassador, Istio, AWS Load Balancer Controller, NGNI, SMI, or Traefik for traffic management, and projects like Prometheus, Datadog, and New Relic to perform analysis to drive progressive delivery.

To install Argo Rollouts to the cluster, run the following command in a terminal window:

```
kubectl create namespace argo-rollouts

kubectl apply -n argo-rollouts -f https://github.com/argoproj/argo-rollouts/relea-
ses/download/v1.2.2/install.yaml
...
clusterrolebinding.rbac.authorization.k8s.io/argo-rollouts created
secret/argo-rollouts-notification-secret created
service/argo-rollouts-metrics created
deployment.apps/argo-rollouts created
```

Although it's not mandatory, we recommend you install the Argo Rollouts Kubectl Plugin to visualize rollouts. Follow the instructions (*https://oreil.ly/1GWsz*) to install it. With everything in place, let's deploy the initial version of the BGD application.

Argo Rollouts doesn't use the standard Kubernetes Deployment file, but a specific new Kubernetes resource named Rollout. It's like a Deployment object, hence all its options are supported, but it adds some fields to configure the rolling update.

Let's deploy the first version of the application. We'll define the canary release process when Kubernetes executes a rolling update, which in this case follows these steps:

1. Forward 20% of traffic to the new version.

2. Wait until a human decides to proceed with the process.

3. Forward 40%, 60%, 80% of the traffic to the new version automatically, waiting 30 seconds between every increase.

Create a new file named *bgd-rollout.yaml* with the following content:

```
apiVersion: argoproj.io/v1alpha1
kind: Rollout
metadata:
  name: bgd-rollouts
spec:
  replicas: 5
  strategy:
    canary: ❶
      steps: ❷
      - setWeight: 20 ❸
      - pause: {} ❹
```

```
        - setWeight: 40
        - pause: {duration: 30s} ❺
        - setWeight: 60
        - pause: {duration: 30s}
        - setWeight: 80
        - pause: {duration: 30s}
    revisionHistoryLimit: 2
    selector:
      matchLabels:
        app: bgd-rollouts
    template: ❻
      metadata:
        creationTimestamp: null
        labels:
          app: bgd-rollouts
      spec:
        containers:
        - image: quay.io/rhdevelopers/bgd:1.0.0
          name: bgd
          env:
          - name: COLOR
            value: "blue"
          resources: {}
```

❶ Canary release

❷ List of steps to execute

❸ Sets the ratio of canary

❹ Rollout is paused

❺ Pauses the rollout for 30 seconds

❻ `template` Deployment definition

Apply the resource to deploy the application. Since there is no previous deployment, the canary part is ignored:

```
kubectl apply -f bgd-rollout.yaml
```

Currently, there are five pods as specified in the `replicas` field:

```
kubectl get pods
```

```
NAME                            READY   STATUS    RESTARTS   AGE
bgd-rollouts-679cdfcfd-6z2zf    1/1     Running   0          12m
bgd-rollouts-679cdfcfd-8c6kl    1/1     Running   0          12m
bgd-rollouts-679cdfcfd-8tb4v    1/1     Running   0          12m
bgd-rollouts-679cdfcfd-f4p7f    1/1     Running   0          12m
bgd-rollouts-679cdfcfd-tljfr    1/1     Running   0          12m
```

And using the Argo Rollout Kubectl Plugin:

```
kubectl argo rollouts get rollout bgd-rollouts
```

```
Name:           bgd-rollouts
Namespace:      default
Status:         ✓ Healthy
Strategy:       Canary
  Step:         8/8
  SetWeight:    100
  ActualWeight: 100
Images:         quay.io/rhdevelopers/bgd:1.0.0 (stable)
Replicas:
  Desired:      5
  Current:      5
  Updated:      5
  Ready:        5
  Available:    5
```

```
NAME                                    KIND         STATUS      AGE  INFO
⟳ bgd-rollouts                          Rollout    ✓ Healthy   13m
└─# revision:1
   └─⊞ bgd-rollouts-679cdfcfd           ReplicaSet ✓ Healthy   13m  stable
      ├─□ bgd-rollouts-679cdfcfd-6z2zf  Pod        ✓ Running   13m  ready:1/1
      ├─□ bgd-rollouts-679cdfcfd-8c6kl  Pod        ✓ Running   13m  ready:1/1
      ├─□ bgd-rollouts-679cdfcfd-8tb4v  Pod        ✓ Running   13m  ready:1/1
      ├─□ bgd-rollouts-679cdfcfd-f4p7f  Pod        ✓ Running   13m  ready:1/1
      └─□ bgd-rollouts-679cdfcfd-tljfr  Pod        ✓ Running   13m  ready:1/1
```

Let's deploy a new version to trigger a canary rolling update. Create a new file named *bgd-rollout-v2.yaml* with exactly the same content as the previous one, but change the environment variable COLOR value to green:

```
...
name: bgd
env:
- name: COLOR
  value: "green"
resources: {}
```

Apply the previous resource and check how Argo Rollouts executes the rolling update. List the pods again to check that 20% of the pods are new while the other 80% are the old version:

```
kubectl get pods
```

```
NAME                             READY  STATUS   RESTARTS  AGE
bgd-rollouts-679cdfcfd-6z2zf     1/1    Running  0         27m
bgd-rollouts-679cdfcfd-8c6kl     1/1    Running  0         27m
bgd-rollouts-679cdfcfd-8tb4v     1/1    Running  0         27m
bgd-rollouts-679cdfcfd-tljfr     1/1    Running  0         27m
bgd-rollouts-c5495c6ff-zfgvn     1/1    Running  0         13s ❶
```

❶ New version pod

And do the same using the Argo Rollout Kubectl Plugin:

```
kubectl argo rollouts get rollout bgd-rollouts
```

```
...
NAME                                    KIND         STATUS       AGE      INFO
⟳ bgd-rollouts                          Rollout      ‖ Paused     31m
├─# revision:2
│   └─⊡ bgd-rollouts-c5495c6ff          ReplicaSet   ✓ Healthy    3m21s    canary
│       └─□ bgd-rollouts-c5495c6ff-zfgvn Pod         ✓ Running    3m21s    ready:1/1
└─# revision:1
    └─⊡ bgd-rollouts-679cdfcfd           ReplicaSet   ✓ Healthy    31m      stable
        ├─□ bgd-rollouts-679cdfcfd-6z2zf Pod          ✓ Running    31m      ready:1/1
        ├─□ bgd-rollouts-679cdfcfd-8c6kl Pod          ✓ Running    31m      ready:1/1
        ├─□ bgd-rollouts-679cdfcfd-8tb4v Pod          ✓ Running    31m      ready:1/1
        └─□ bgd-rollouts-679cdfcfd-tljfr Pod          ✓ Running    31m      ready:1/1
```

Remember that the rolling update process is paused until the operator executes a manual step to let the process continue. In a terminal window, run the following command:

```
kubectl argo rollouts promote bgd-rollouts
```

The rollout is promoted and continues with the following steps, which is substituting the old version pods with new versions every 30 seconds:

```
kubectl get pods
```

```
NAME                            READY   STATUS    RESTARTS   AGE
bgd-rollouts-c5495c6ff-2g7r8    1/1     Running   0          89s
bgd-rollouts-c5495c6ff-7mdch    1/1     Running   0          122s
bgd-rollouts-c5495c6ff-d9828    1/1     Running   0          13s
bgd-rollouts-c5495c6ff-h4t6f    1/1     Running   0          56s
bgd-rollouts-c5495c6ff-zfgvn    1/1     Running   0          11m
```

The rolling update finishes with the new version progressively deployed to the cluster.

Discussion

Kubernetes doesn't implement advanced deployment techniques natively. For this reason, Argo Rollouts uses the number of deployed pods to implement the canary release.

As mentioned before, Argo Rollouts integrates with Kubernetes products that offer advanced traffic management capabilities like Istio (*https://istio.io*).

Using Istio, the traffic splitting is done correctly at the infrastructure level instead of playing with replica numbers like in the first example. Argo Rollouts integrates with Istio to execute a canary release, automatically updating the Istio `VirtualService` object.

Assuming you already know Istio and have a Kubernetes cluster with Istio installed, you can perform integration between Argo Rollouts and Istio by setting the trafficRouting from Rollout resource to Istio.

First, create a Rollout file with Istio configured:

```
apiVersion: argoproj.io/v1alpha1
kind: Rollout
metadata:
  name: bgdapp
  labels:
    app: bgdapp
spec:
  strategy:
    canary: ❶
      steps:
      - setWeight: 20
      - pause:
          duration: "1m"
      - setWeight: 50
      - pause:
          duration: "2m"
      canaryService: bgd-canary ❷
      stableService: bgd ❸
      trafficRouting:
        istio: ❹
          virtualService: ❺
            name: bgd ❻
            routes:
            - primary ❼
  replicas: 1
  revisionHistoryLimit: 2
  selector:
    matchLabels:
      app: bgdapp
      version: v1
  template:
    metadata:
      labels:
        app: bgdapp
        version: v1
      annotations:
        sidecar.istio.io/inject: "true" ❽
    spec:
      containers:
      - image: quay.io/rhdevelopers/bgd:1.0.0
        name: bgd
        env:
        - name: COLOR
          value: "blue"
        resources: {}
```

❶ Canary section

❷ Reference to a Kubernetes Service pointing to the new service version

❸ Reference to a Kubernetes Service pointing to the old service version

❹ Configures Istio

❺ Reference to the VirtualService where weight is updated

❻ Name of the VirtualService

❼ Route name within VirtualService

❽ Deploys the Istio sidecar container

Then, we create two Kubernetes Services pointing to the same deployment used to redirect traffic to the old or the new one.

The following Kubernetes Service is used in the stableService field:

```
apiVersion: v1
kind: Service
metadata:
  name: bgd
  labels:
    app: bgdapp
spec:
  ports:
  - name: http
    port: 8080
  selector:
    app: bgdapp
```

And the Canary one is the same but with a different name. It's the one used in the canaryService field:

```
apiVersion: v1
kind: Service
metadata:
  name: bgd-canary
  labels:
    app: bgdapp
spec:
  ports:
  - name: http
    port: 8080
  selector:
    app: bgdapp
```

Finally, create the Istio Virtual Service to be updated by Argo Rollouts to update the canary traffic for each service:

```
apiVersion: networking.istio.io/v1alpha3
kind: VirtualService
metadata:
  name: bgd
spec:
  hosts:
  - bgd
  http:
  - route:
    - destination:
        host: bgd ❶
      weight: 100
    - destination:
        host: bgd-canary ❷
      weight: 0
    name: primary ❸
```

❶ Stable Kubernetes Service

❷ Canary Kubernetes Service

❸ Route name

After applying these resources, we'll get the first version of the application up and running:

```
kubectl apply -f bgd-virtual-service.yaml
kubectl apply -f service.yaml
kubectl apply -f service-canary.yaml
kubectl apply -f bgd-isio-rollout.yaml
```

When any update occurs on the Rollout object, the canary release will start as described in the Solution. Now, Argo Rollouts updates the *bgd virtual service* weights automatically instead of playing with pod numbers.

See Also

- Argo Rollouts - Kubernetes Progressive Delivery Controller (*https://oreil.ly/XQ64b*)
- Istio - Argo Rollouts (*https://oreil.ly/lKDYH*)
- Istio (*https://istio.io*)
- Istio Tutorial from Red Hat (*https://oreil.ly/Vzk9G*)

Index

About the Authors

Natale Vinto is a software engineer with more than 10 years of expertise in IT and ICT technologies and a consolidated background in Telecommunications and Linux operating systems. As a solution architect with a Java development background, he spent some years as an EMEA Specialist Solution Architect for OpenShift at Red Hat. He is coauthor of *Modernizing Enterprise Java* for O'Reilly. Today Natale is lead developer advocate at Red Hat, helping people within communities and customers have success with their Kubernetes and cloud native strategy. You can follow more frequent updates on his Twitter feed (*https://twitter.com/natalevinto*) and connect with him on LinkedIn (*https://www.linkedin.com/in/natalevinto*).

Alex Soto Bueno is a director of developer experience at Red Hat. He is passionate about the Java world, software automation, and he believes in the open source software model. Alex is the coauthor of *Testing Java Microservices* (Manning), *Quarkus Cookbook* (O'Reilly), and the forthcoming *Kubernetes Secrets Management* (Manning), and is a contributor to several open source projects. A Java Champion since 2017, he is also an international speaker and teacher at Salle URL University. You can follow more frequent updates on his Twitter feed (*https://twitter.com/alexsotob*) and connect with him on LinkedIn (*https://www.linkedin.com/in/asotobu*).

Colophon

The animal on the cover of *GitOps Cookbook* is a yellow mongoose (*Cynictis penicillata*). These small mammals are found in sub-Saharan Africa, primarily in forests, woodlands, grasslands, and scrub. They are sometimes referred to as red meerkats. Yellow mongoose are smaller than most other species, weighing only 16–29 ounces. There are 12 subspecies that vary in color, body size (9–13 inches), tail (7–10 inches), and length of coat: the northern subspecies found in Botswana are typically smaller with grizzled grayish coats while the southern populations in South Africa and Namibia are larger and tawny yellow. All subspecies have slender bodies with lighter fur on the chin and underbelly, small ears, pointed noses, and bushy tails.

Yellow mongoose are carnivores that mainly feed on insects, birds, frogs, lizards, eggs and small rodents. They are social species and live in colonies of up to 20 individuals in extensive, permanent burrows with many entrances, chambers, and tunnels. Most of their day is spent foraging or sunbathing outside the burrow. In the wild, they breed from July to September with most females giving birth to two or three offspring in October and November. The young are born in an underground chamber and stay there until they are weaned (about 10 weeks). Yellow mongoose are considered fully grown at 10 months old.

Yellow mongoose are classified as a species of least concern by the IUCN; their populations are stable and they don't face any major threats. They do carry of strain of rabies in the wild and are seen as pests and hunted by farmers in parts of South Africa. Many of the animals on O'Reilly covers are endangered; all of them are important to the world.

The cover illustration is by Karen Montgomery, based on an antique line engraving from *The Pictorial Museum of Animated Nature*. The cover fonts are Gilroy Semibold and Guardian Sans. The text font is Adobe Minion Pro; the heading font is Adobe Myriad Condensed; and the code font is Dalton Maag's Ubuntu Mono.

O'REILLY®

Learn from experts.
Become one yourself.

Books | Live online courses
Instant Answers | Virtual events
Videos | Interactive learning

Get started at oreilly.com.